THE

VULGATE

LATIN COURSE:

CONTAINING

GRAMMAR, DELECTUS, EXERCISE BOOK, AND VOCABULARIES.

FOR THE USE OF SCHOOLS.

BY

WILLIAM DODDS,

MASTER OF WRAGBY GRAMMAR SCHOOL;

Author of "The Excelsior Latin Series," "A Complete Guide to Matriculation at the University of London," "Algebra for Beginners," &c.

MANCHESTER: JOHN HEYWOOD, 141 AND 143, DEANSGATE;
EDUCATIONAL DEPARTMENT, 141, DEANSGATE.
LONDON: SIMPKIN, MARSHALL, & CO.; J. C. TACEY.

PREFACE.

THE plan of the following work was suggested by M. Arnold, Esq., one of Her Majesty's Inspectors of Schools, in his General Report of the Public Elementary Schools visited by him in the Westminster Division during the year 1871–2. He expresses a hope that Latin will be much more used as a special subject, and even adopted, finally, as part of the regular instruction in the upper classes of all Elementary Schools. "Of course I mean," he says, "Latin studied in a very simple way; but I am more and more struck with the stimulating and instructing effect upon a child's mind of possessing a second language, in however limited a degree, as an object of reference and comparison; and Latin is the foundation of so much in the written and spoken language of modern Europe, that it is the best to take as a second language." Mr. Arnold is of opinion, however, that the teaching should be on quite a different plan from that adopted in classical schools: "I am convinced that, for the elementary teacher's purpose, the best way would be to disregard classical Latin entirely; to use neither 'Cornelius Nepos,' nor 'Eutropius,' nor 'Cæsar,' nor any *delectus* from them, but to use the Latin Bible, the Vulgate. A chapter or two from the story of Joseph, a chapter or two from Deuteronomy, and the first two chapters of St. Luke's Gospel, would be the sort of *delectus* we want; add to them a vocabulary, and a simple grammar of the main forms of the Latin language, and you have a perfectly compact and cheap school book, and yet all that you need. In the extracts the child would be at home, instead of, as in extracts from classical Latin, in an utterly strange land; and the Latin of the Vulgate, while it is real and living Latin, is yet, like the Greek of the New Testament, much nearer to modern idiom, and, therefore, much easier for a modern learner than classical idiom can be. * * * What we want to give to our elementary schools in general is the vocabulary, to some extent, of a second language, and that language one which is at the bottom of a great deal of modern life and modern language."

The plan thus roughly sketched by Mr. Arnold we have here endeavoured to carry out.

PART I. contains an outline of the Accidence and the First Rules of Syntax, with exercises in Declension and Conjugation to be written out and committed to memory.

PART II. consists of a collection of easy and familiar extracts from the Latin Bible, preceded by a few simple exercises for parsing and construing on the principal rules of grammar, progressively arranged, and gradually leading up to the Sacred Text, which may be used *pari passu* with the Grammar, or their study deferred until the pupil has made some progress with the Accidence, at the discretion of the teacher.

PART III. contains a number of easy, simple sentences for translation into Latin, based upon the introductory exercises in Part II.

The study of Latin is one which is generally admitted to be of the highest importance, and hence we find that it occupies a foremost place in the *curriculum* of every school having any pretension to respectability. And rightly so, for it forms an excellent mental discipline, and is admirably adapted for sharpening the wits, strengthening the memory, and cultivating the judgment, thereby increasing the student's general capacity for work ; whilst from Latin, more than any other language, can we gain a knowledge of the general laws of grammar, upon which all languages are built. But the main advantage to be derived from a knowledge of Latin is the immense assistance it affords us to a correct spelling of English. In fact, it offers us a complete key to the spelling of a large number of the very words with which children and those unacquainted with the grammatical structure of the Roman tongue experience most difficulty. At least ten thousand words in the English language, many of them in common use, are of Latin origin, and cannot readily be understood by those ignorant of the originals ; whereas a slight knowledge of Latin would give a clue to the root-words and the prepositions by which their compounds are formed, and lay bare their meaning at once. The importance of these roots may be seen from the fact that "from *pono* and *positum* we have in English two hundred and fifty words ; from *plico* two hundred ; from *fero* and *latum* one hundred and ninety-eight ; from *specio* one hundred and seventy-seven ; from *mitto* and *missum* one hundred and seventy-four ; from *teneo* and *tentum* one hundred and sixty-eight ; from *capio* and *captum* one hundred and ninety-seven ; from *tendo* and *tensum* one hundred and sixty-two ; from *duco* and *ductum* one hundred and fifty-six ;" that is to say, from nine Latin verbs are derived sixteen hundred and eighty-two English words. Teachers of Elementary Schools will therefore find this a most useful extra subject, that will not only prove "easy to learn and pleasant to teach," but will also indirectly increase the money grants for Reading and Dictation, whilst very little time need be devoted to it in school, as the rules of grammar and the vocabularies can all be learnt at home.

§§ 1—32 are adapted to the requirements of Standard IV. ; §§ 33—77, 81—137, and Exercises I.—XXIV. for Standard V. ; the remainder of the work for Standard VI.

THE VULGATE LATIN COURSE.

Part I.—GRAMMAR.

THE ALPHABET AND PARTS OF SPEECH.

§ 1. The Latin ALPHABET consists of 25 letters, the same as the English without *W*, both capitals and small.

§ 2. The LETTERS are divided into vowels and consonants.

§ 3. The VOWELS are *a, e, i, o, u, y;* the rest are Consonants.

§ 4. A SYLLABLE consists of one or more letters pronounced together. Every syllable contains at least one vowel.

A DIPHTHONG is the sound of two vowels in one syllable.

The Latin diphthongs are **ae, *oe, au,* and *ei, eu, ui.*

A syllable is long (ā) or short (ă), according to the length (or quantity) of its vowel.

OBS.—All syllables containing a diphthong are long.

§ 5. The PARTS OF SPEECH are eight, viz. : Noun, Pronoun, Adjective, Verb, Adverb, Preposition, Conjunction, Interjection.

NOTE.—There is no Article in Latin, so that *nox* may be translated "night," "a night," or "the night."

(1) NOUNS are the names of persons, places, and things ; as *Paulus*, St. Paul ; *Galilaea*, Galilee ; *mensa*, a table.

---

* These diphthongs are often printed thus: Æ, æ : Œ, œ, and are sounded like "e" in the English word "me," as in *Cæsar.*

600096213R

(2) PRONOUNS stand instead of Nouns; as *ego*, I; *tu*, thou; *ille*, he.

(3) ADJECTIVES express the qualities of persons and things; as, *unus dives et alter pauper*, the one rich and the other poor.

(4) VERBS tell what persons and things do, suffer, or are; as, *scribae dicunt*, the scribes say; *agnus occisus est*, a lamb was slain; *lex est bona*, the law is good.

(5) ADVERBS show how, when, or where a thing is done; as, *Venio cito*, I come quickly.

(6) PREPOSITIONS govern the cases of nouns and pronouns, and show their relation to each other; as, *Vado ad Patrem*, I go to the Father.

(7) CONJUNCTIONS join together words and sentences: as, *oves et boves*, sheep and oxen.

(8) INTERJECTIONS are words of exclamation; as, *Ecce Homo!* Behold the man!

§ 6. Nouns, Pronouns, Adjectives, and Verbs are inflected, *i.e.*, their endings are changed in order to show their relation to other words, where we in English use prepositions, by, with, from, in, to, for, &c.

The inflection of Nouns, Pronouns, and Adjectives is called DECLENSION; that of Verbs, CONJUGATION.

NOUNS.

§ 7. Nouns are declined by Number and Case.

There are two numbers, Singular and Plural. The SINGULAR speaks of one, and the PLURAL of more than one; as *discipulus* (sing.), a disciple; *discipuli* (plur.), disciples.

§ 8. There are six CASES, Nominative, Genitive, Dative, Accusative, Vocative, Ablative.

(1) The NOMINATIVE CASE usually goes before the verb, and answers the question Who? or What? As, Who sleeps? ANS., *Puella dormit*, the maid sleepeth.

(2) The GENITIVE CASE is translated by, of, or 's, and answers the question whose? As, Whose son? ANS., *fabri filius*, the carpenter's son.

(3) The DATIVE CASE answers the question *to* or *for whom* or *what?* As, To whom was it given? ANS., *Datum est puellae*, it was given to the damsel.

(4) The ACCUSATIVE CASE generally follows the verb, and answers the question *whom* or *what?* As, Whom does the Father love? ANS., *Pater amat Filium*, the Father loveth the Son.

(5) The VOCATIVE CASE is translated by O ; as *Mi fili*, O my son.

(6) The ABLATIVE CASE is translated by the prepositions *by, with, from, in*, and others; as, *In domo Patris mei*, in my Father's house.

§ 9. All Latin Nouns are arranged in five classes, called DECLENSIONS, distinguished by the endings of the Genitive Case Singular :—

(1) ae,   (2) ĭ,   (3) ĭs,   (4) ūs,   (5) ĕi.

§ 10. There are Three GENDERS, Masculine, Feminine, Neuter.

OBS.—When a noun may be either Masculine or Feminine, it is said to be of the Common Gender ; as *parens*, parent.

FIRST DECLENSION.

§ 11. The Nominative Singular of Nouns of the First Declension ends in *a*, and the Genitive in *ae*.

	Singular.			Plural.	
Nom.	Mens-ă,	*a table*	Mens-ae,	*tables*	
Gen.	Mens-ae,	*of a table*	Mens-ārum,	*of tables*	
Dat.	Mens-ae,	*to, or for a table*	Mens-Is,	*to, or for tables*	
Acc.	Mens-am,	*a table*	Mens-ās,	*tables*	
Voc.	Mens-ă,	*O table [a table.*	Mens-ae,	*O tables [tables.*	
Abl.	Mens-ă,	*by, with, or from*	Mens-Is,	*by, with, or from*	

OBS.—Every noun is made up of two parts ; (1) the STEM, that part of the word which remains unchanged ; and (2) the CASE-ENDING. The stem of a noun may always be found by throwing away the case-ending of the gen. sing. Stem, *mens*. Case-endings *a, ae, am, arum, is, as*.

Nouns of the First Declension are Feminine, except the names of males, as *Poeta*, a poet ; *Propheta*, a prophet.

Decline also ; *Turba*, a multitude ; *puella*, a girl ; *causa*, a cause ; *scriba*, a scribe ; *poeta*, a poet ; *porta*, a gate ; *propheta*, a prophet ; *flamma*, a flame ; *stella*, a star ; *epistola*, a letter.

SECOND DECLENSION.

§ 12. The Nominative Singular of Nouns of the Second Declension ends in *us, er, um,* and the Genitive in *i.*

Nouns in *us* and *er* are generally Masculine, those in *um* Neuter.

A. *Masculine.*

Singular.

	Singular.		**1.** Plural.	
Nom.	**Dŏmĭn-ŭs,**	*the lord*	**Dŏmĭn-ī,**	*lords*
Gen.	**Dŏmĭn-ī,**	*of the lord*	**Dŏmĭn-ōrum,**	*of lords*
Dat.	**Dŏmĭn-ō,**	*to, or for the lord*	**Dŏmĭn-īs,**	*to, or for lords*
Acc.	**Dŏmĭn-um,**	*the lord*	**Dŏmĭn-ōs,**	*lords*
Voc.	**Dŏmĭn-ĕ,**	*0 lord [the lord.*	**Dŏmĭn-ī,**	*0. lords [lords.*
Abl.	**Dŏmĭn-ō,**	*by, with,* or *from*	**Dŏmĭn-īs,**	*by, with,* or *from*

2.

Nom.	**Măgĭstĕr,**	*a master*	**Măgĭstr-ī,**	*masters*
Gen.	**Măgĭstr-ī,**	*of a master*	**Măgĭstr-ōrum,**	*of masters*
Dat.	**Măgĭstr-ō,**	*to, or for a master*	**Măgĭstr-īs,**	*to, or for masters*
Acc.	**Măgĭstr-um,**	*a master*	**Măgĭstr-ōs,**	*masters*
Voc.	**Măgĭstĕr,**	*0 master*	**Măgĭstr-ī,**	*0 masters*
Abl.	**Măgĭstr-ō,**	*by, with,* or *from a master.*	**Măgĭstr-īs,**	*by, with,* or *from masters.*

3.

Nom.	**Pŭĕr,**	*a boy*	**Pŭĕr-ī,**	*boys*
Gen	**Pŭĕr-ī,**	*of a boy*	**Pŭĕr-ōrum,**	*of boys*
Dat.	**Pŭĕr-ō,**	*to, or for a boy*	**Pŭĕr-īs,**	*to, or for boys*
Acc.	**Pŭĕr-um,**	*a boy*	**Pŭĕr-ōs,**	*boys*
Voc.	**Pŭĕr,**	*0 boy [a boy.*	**Pŭĕr-ī,**	*0 boys [boys.*
Abl.	**Pŭĕr-ō,**	*by, with,* or *from*	**Pŭĕr-īs,**	*by, with,* or *from*

B. *Neuter.*

	Singular.		Plural.	
Nom.	**Regn-um,**	*a kingdom*	**Regn-ā,**	*kingdoms*
Gen.	**Regn-ī,**	*of a kingdom*	**Regn-ōrum,**	*of kingdoms*
Dat.	**Regn-ō,**	*to or for a kingdom*	**Regn-īs,**	*to or for kingdoms*
Acc.	**Regn-um,**	*a kingdom*	**Regn-ā,**	*kingdoms*
Voc.	**Regn-um,**	*0 kingdom*	**Regn-ā,**	*0 kingdoms*
Abl.	**Regn-ō,**	*by, with,* or *from a kingdom.*	**Regn-īs,**	*by, with,* or *from kingdoms.*

Obs.—1. The Nominative, Accusative, and Vocative of all Neuter Nouns are alike in each number, and in the Plural these Cases always end in *a*.

2. The Vocative is always the same as the Nominative, except iu Singular Nouns of the Second Declension in *us*. The Dative and Ablative Plural are always the same.

3. *Filius*, a son, makes *fili* in the Vocative Singular.

4. Most Nouns in *er* are declined like *magister*, throwing out *e* in the Genitive, a few only are declined like *puer*.

Decline also (like *Dominus*):—*Angelus*, an angel; *inimicus*, an enemy; *hortus*, a garden; *gladius*, a sword; *murus*, a wall; *servus*, a servant: *asinus*, an ass; *amicus*, a friend; *oculus*, an eye; *annus*, a year; *discipulus*, a disciple; *lupus*, a wolf; *agnus*, a lamb; *digitus*, a finger; *equus*, a horse.

Decline also (like *Magister*):—*Minister*, *ministri*, a servant; *faber*, *fabri*, a workman (a carpenter); *liber*, *libri*, a book; *ager*, *agri*, a field; *arbiter*, *arbitri*, an umpire.

Decline also (like *Puer*):—*Socer*, *soceri*, a father-in-law; *gener*, *generi*, a son-in-law; *vesper*, *vesperi*, evening.

Decline also (like *Regnum*):—*Bellum*, war; *astrum*, a star; *donum*, a gift; *jugum*, a yoke; *pretium*, value, price; *vestigium*, footstep; *templum*, a temple; *signum*, a sign; *folium*, a leaf; *verbum*, a word; *coelum*, heaven; *proelium*, a battle; *scutum*, a shield.

THIRD DECLENSION.

§ 13. The Nominative Singular of Nouns of the Third Declension ends in various letters, but the Genitive Singular always ends in *is*.

A. *Masculine* and *Feminine*.

(a) Not increasing in the Genitive.*

Singular.		1.	Plural.	
Nom.	**Nūb-ĕs**, a cloud		**Nūb-ĕs**, clouds	
Gen.	**Nūb-ĭs**, of a cloud		**Nūb-ĭum**, of clouds	
Dat.	**Nūb-ī**, to or for a cloud		**Nūb-ĭbŭs**, to or for clouds	
Acc.	**Nūb-em**, a cloud		**Nūb-ĕs**, clouds	
Voc.	**Nūb-ĕs**, O cloud [cloud.		**Nūb-ĕs**, O clouds	
Abl.	**Nūb-ĕ**, by, with, or from a		**Nūb-ĭbŭs**, by, with, or from clouds.	

* When the Genitive Singular contains a syllable more than the Nominative, the Noun is said to increase in the Genitive.

	Singular.		2.	Plural.
Nom.	Cīv-ĭs,	a citizen	Cīv-ĕs,	citizens
Gen.	Cīv-ĭs,	of a citizen	Cīv-ĭum,	of citizens
Dat.	Cīv-ī,	to or for a citizen	Cīv-ĭbŭs,	to or for citizens
Acc.	Cīv-em,	a citizen	Cīv-ĕs,	citizens
Voc.	Cīv-ĭs,	O citizen [citizen.	Cīv-ĕs,	O citizens
Abl.	Cīv-ĕ,	by, with, or from a	Cīv-ĭbŭs,	by, with, or from citizens.

(b) Increasing in the Genitive.

1.

Nom.	Lăpĭs,	a stone	Lăpĭd-ĕs,	stones
Gen.	Lăpĭd-ĭs,	of a stone	Lăpĭd-um,	of stones
Dat.	Lăpĭd-ī,	to or for a stone	Lăpĭd-ĭbŭs,	to or for stones
Acc.	Lăpĭd-em,	a stone	Lăpĭd-ĕs,	stones
Voc.	Lăpĭs,	O stone [a stone.	Lăpĭd-ĕs,	O stones [stones.
Abl.	Lăpĭd-ĕ,	by, with, or from	Lăpĭd-ĭbŭs,	by, with, or from

2.

Nom.	Jūdex,	a judge	Jūdĭc-ĕs,	judges
Gen.	Jūdĭc-ĭs,	of a judge	Jūdĭc-um,	of judges
Dat.	Jūdĭc-ī,	to or for a judge	Jūdĭc-ĭbŭs,	to or for judges
Acc.	Jūdĭc-em,	a judge	Jūdĭc-ĕs,	judges
Voc.	Jūdex,	O judge [a judge.	Jūdĭc-ĕs,	O judges [judges.
Abl.	Jūdĭc-ĕ,	by, with, or from	Jūdĭc-ĭbŭs,	by, with, or from

3.

Nom.	Virgŏ,	a virgin	Virgĭn-ĕs,	virgins
Gen.	Virgĭn-ĭs,	of a virgin	Virgĭn-um,	of virgins
Dat.	Virgĭn-ī,	to or for a virgin	Virgĭn-ĭbŭs,	to or for virgins
Acc.	Virgĭn-em,	a virgin	Virgĭn-ĕs,	virgins
Voc.	Virgŏ,	O virgin	Virgĭn-ĕs,	O virgins
Abl.	Virgĭn-ĕ,	by, with, or from a virgin.	Virgĭn-ĭbŭs,	by, with, or from virgins.

4.

Nom.	Sěrpēns,	a serpent	Sěrpěnt-ĕs,	serpents
Gen.	Sěrpěnt-ĭs,	of a serpent	Sěrpěnt-ĭum,	of serpents
Dat.	Sěrpěnt-ī,	to or for a serpent	Sěrpěnt-ĭbŭs,	to or for serpents
Acc.	Sěrpěnt-em,	a serpent	Sěrpěnt-ĕs,	serpents
Voc.	Sěrpēns,	O serpent	Sěrpěnt-ĕs,	O serpents
Abl.	Sěrpěnt-ĕ,	by, with, or from a serpent.	Sěrpěnt-ĭbŭs,	by, with, or from serpents.

B. *Neuters.*

(*a*) Plural *a.*

1.

	Singular.			Plural.	
Nom.	Nŏmĕn,	*a name*	Nŏmĭn-ă,	*names*
Gen.	Nŏmĭn-ĭs,	*of a name*	Nŏmĭn-um,	*of names*
Dat.	Nŏmĭn-ī,	*to or for a name*	Nŏmĭnĭ-būs,	*to or for names*
Acc.	Nŏmĕn,	*a name*	Nŏmĭn-ă,	*names*
Voc.	Nŏmĕn,	*O name [a name.*	Nŏmĭn-ă,	*O names　[names.*
Abl.	Nŏmĭn-ĕ,	*by, with, or from*	Nŏmĭn-ĭbūs,	*by, with, or from*

2.

Nom.	Opŭs,	*a work*	Opĕr-ă,	*works*
Gen.	Opĕr-ĭs,	*of a work*	Opĕr-um,	*of works*
Dat.	Opĕr-ī,	*to or for a work*	Opĕr-ĭbūs,	*to or for works*
Acc.	Opŭs,	*a work*	Opĕr-ă,	*works*
Voc.	Opŭs,	*O work　[work.*	Opĕr-ă.	*O works*
Abl.	Opĕr-ĕ,	*by, with, or from a*	Opĕr-ĭbūs,	*by, with, or from works*

(*b*) Plural *ia.*

1.

Nom.	Mărĕ,	*the sea*	Măr-Iă,	*seas*
Gen.	Măr-Is,	*of the sea*	Măr-Ium,	*of seas*
Dat.	Măr-I,	*to or for the sea*	Măr-Ibūs,	*to or for seas*
Acc.	Mărĕ,	*the sea*	Măr-Iă,	*seas*
Voc.	Mărĕ,	*O sea　[sea.*	Măr-Iă,	*O seas*
Abl.	Măr-I,	*by, with, or from the*	Măr-Ibūs,	*by, with, or from seas.*

2.

Nom.	Anĭmăl,	*an animal*	Anĭmăl-Iă,	*animals*
Gen.	Anĭmăl-Is,	*of an animal*	Anĭmăl-Ium,	*of animals*
Dat.	Anĭmăl-I,	*to or for an animal*	Anĭmăl-Ibūs,	*to or for animals*
Acc.	Anĭmăl,	*an animal*	Anĭmăl-Iă,	*animals*
Voc.	Anĭmăl,	*O animal*	Anĭmăl-Iă,	*O animals*
Abl.	Anĭmăl-I,	*by, with, or from an animal.*	Anĭmăl-Ibūs,	*by, with, or from animals.*

Decline also (like *Nubes*) :—*Auris, auris,* an ear ; *testis, testis,* a witness *ovis, ovis,* a sheep ; *avis, avis,* a bird ; *pars, partis,* a part ; *nox, noctis,* night ; *urbs, urbis,* a city ; *civis, civis,* a citizen.

Decline also (like *Lapis*) :—*Rex, regis,* a king ; *princeps, principis,* a chief ; *flos, floris,* a flower ; *pes, pedis,* a foot ; *trabs, trabis,* a beam ; *arbor, arboris,* a tree ; *sacerdos, sacerdotis,* a priest ; *lex, legis,* a law ; *homo, hominis,* a man ; *leo, leonis,* a lion ; *miles, militis,* a soldier.

Decline also (like *Serpens*) :—*Gens, gentis,* a nation ; *mons, montis,* a mountain; *dens, dentis,* a tooth ; *pons, pontis,* a bridge ; *fons, fontis,* a fountain.

Decline also (like *Nomen*) :—*Corpus, corporis,* a body ; *caput, capitis,* a head ; *cor, cordis,* a heart ; *tempus, temporis,* time ; *munus, muneris,* a gift ; *onus, oneris,* a burden ; *carmen, carminis,* a song.

Decline also (like *Mare*) :—*Rete, retis,* a net ; *altare, altaris,* an altar.

FOURTH DECLENSION.

§ 14. The Nominative Singular of Masculine and Feminine Nouns of the Fourth Declension ends in *us*, Neuters in *u*.

1.

	Singular.		Plural.
Nom.	**Grăd-ŭs,** *a step*	**Grăd-ūs,**	*steps*
Gen.	**Grăd-ūs,** *of a step*	**Grăd-ŭum.**	*of steps*
Dat.	**Grăd-ŭī,** *to or for a step*	**Grăd-ĭbŭs,**	*to or for steps*
Acc.	**Grăd-um,** *a step*	**Grăd-ūs,**	*steps*
Voc.	**Grăd-ŭs,** *O step* [*a step.*	**Grăd-ūs,**	*O steps*
Abl.	**Grăd-ū,** *by, with,* or *from*	**Grăd-ĭbŭs,**	*by, with,* or *from steps.*

2.

Nom.	**Gĕn-u,** *a knee*	**Gĕn-ŭă,**	*knees*
Gen.	**Gĕn-ūs,** *of a knee*	**Gĕn-ŭum,**	*of knees*
Dat.	**Gĕn-ū,** *to or for a knee*	**Gĕn-ĭbŭs,**	*to or for knees*
Acc.	**Gĕn-ū,** *a knee*	**Gĕn-ŭă,**	*knees*
Voc.	**Gĕn-ū,** *O knee* [*knee.*	**Gĕn-ŭă,**	*O knees*
Abl.	**Gĕn u,** *by, with,* or *from a*	**Gĕn-ĭbŭs,**	*by, with,* or *from knees.*

Obs.--The holy name of JESUS is thus declined : N. *Jesus,* G. D. V. and Abl. *Jesu,* Acc. *Jesum.*

Decline also (like *Gradus*) :—*Fructus,* fruit ; *manus,* the hand ; *exercitus,* an army ; *spiritus,* a spirit ; *portus,* a haven ; *passus,* a pace ; *quercus*,* an oak ; *tribus*,* a tribe.

Decline also (like *Genu*) : *Cornu,* a horn.

---

*Ablative Plural—*ubus.*

FIFTH DECLENSION.

§ 15. The Nominative Singular of Nouns of the Fifth Declension ends in *es*, and the Genitive in *ei*.

Singular.			Plural.	
Nom.	DI-ĕs,	*a day*	DI-ĕs,	*days*
Gen.	DI-ĕī,	*of a day*	DI-ōrum,	*of days*
Dat.	DI-ĕī,	*to or for a day*	DI-ĕbŭs,	*to or for days*
Acc.	DI-em,	*a day*	DI-ĕs,	*days*
Voc.	DI-ĕs,	*0 day* [*day.*	DI-ĕs,	*0 days*
Abl.	DI-ĕ,	*by, with, or from a*	DI-ĕbŭs,	*by, with, or from days.*

Obs.—Nouns of the Fifth Declension are Feminine, except *Dies*, which is Common in the Singular, and Masculine in the Plural.

Decline also (like *Dies*) :—*Facies*, a face ; *res*, a thing ; and, in Singular only, *species*, appearance ; *spes*, hope ; *fides*, faith.

IRREGULAR NOUNS.

§ 16. The following are irregularly declined:—*Vir*, a man, or husband ; *vis*, strength ; *domus*, a house ; *bos*, an ox ; *senex*, an old man ; *Deus*, God.

S. Nom.	Vĭr (*man*)	VIs (*strength*)	Domŭs (*house*)	
Gen.	Vĭrī	—	Domūs	
Dat.	Vĭrō	—	Domŭī	
Acc.	Vĭrum	Vim	Domum	
Voc.	Vĭr	—	Domŭs	
Abl.	Vĭrŏ	VI	Domo	
P. Nom.	Vĭrī	Vĭrĕs	Domŭs	
Gen.	Vĭrōrum	Vĭrĭum	Domŭum (domōrum)	
Dat.	Vĭrīs	Vĭrĭbŭs	Domĭbŭs	
Acc.	Vĭrŏs	Vĭrĕs	Domŏs (domūs)	
Voc.	Vĭrī	Vĭrĕs	Domŭs	
Abl.	Vĭrīs	Vĭrĭbŭs	Domĭbŭs	

The form *domi* is used to signify "at home."

S. Nom.	Bŏs (*ox*)	Sĕnex (*old man*)	Dĕŭs (*God*)
Gen.	Bŏvĭs	Sĕnĭs	Deī
Dat.	Bŏvī	Sĕnī	Deō
Acc.	Bŏvem	Sĕnem	Deum
Voc.	Bŏs	Sĕnex	Dĕŭs
Abl.	Bŏvĕ	Sĕnĕ	Deō
P. Nom.	Bŏvĕs	Sĕnĕs	Deī, Dĭī, Dī
Gen.	Bŏvum (bŏum)	Sĕnum	Deōrum, Deûm
Dat.	Bŏbŭs (bûbŭs)	Sĕnĭbŭs	Deīs, Dĭīs, Dīs
Acc.	Bŏvĕs	Sĕnĕs	Deōs
Voc.	Bŏvĕs	Sĕnĕs	Deī, Dĭī, Dī
Abl.	Bŏbŭs (bûbŭs)	Sĕnĭbŭs	Deīs, Dĭīs, Dīs

ADJECTIVES.

§ 17. Adjectives are declined by Number, Gender, and Case.

§ 18. Adjectives of Three Endings in *us, a, um,* or *er, a, um,* follow the First and Second Declensions of Nouns; as, *bonus,* good; *niger,* black; *tener,* tender.

Bonus, a, um, are declined like *Dominus, Mensa,* and *Regnum.*

Niger is declined like *Magister,* and *Tener* like *Puer.*

	Singular.		1.		Plural.	
M.	F.	N.		M.	F.	N.
N. Bŏnŭs	bŏnă	bŏnum		Bŏnī	bŏnae	bŏnă
G. Bŏnī	bŏnae	bŏnī		Bŏnōrum	bŏnārum	bŏnōrum
D. Bŏnō	bŏnae	bŏnō		Bŏnīs	bŏnīs	bŏnīs
A. Bŏnum	bŏnam	bŏnum		Bŏnōs	bŏnās	bŏnă
V. Bŏnĕ	bŏnă	bŏnum		Bŏnī	bŏnae	bŏnă
A. Bonō	bŏnă	bŏnō		Bŏnīs	bŏnīs	bŏnīs

			2.			
N. Nĭgĕr	nigră	nigrum		Nĭgrī	nigrae	nigră
G. Nĭgrī	nigrae	nigrī		Nĭgrōrum	nigrārum	nigrōrum
D. Nĭgrō	nigrae	nigr-ō		Nĭgrīs	nigrīs	nigrīs
A. Nĭgrum	nigram	nigrum		Nĭgrōs	nigrās	nigră
V. Nĭgĕr	nigră	nigrum		Nĭgrī	nigrae	nigră
A. Nĭgrō	nigră	nigrō		Nĭgrīs	nigrīs	nigrīs

			3.			
N. Tĕnĕr	tĕnĕră	tĕnĕrum		Tĕnĕrī	tĕnĕrae	tĕnĕră
G. Tĕnĕrī	tĕnĕrae	tĕnĕrī		Tĕnĕrōrum	tĕnĕrārum	tĕnĕrōrum
D. Tĕnĕrō	tĕnĕrae	tĕnĕrō		Tĕnĕrīs	tĕnĕrīs	tĕnĕrīs
A. Tĕnĕrum	tĕnĕram	tĕnĕrum		Tĕnĕrōs	tĕnĕrās	tĕnĕră
V. Tĕnĕr	tĕnĕră	tĕnĕrum		Tĕnĕrī	tĕnĕrae	tĕnĕră
A. Tĕnĕrō	tĕnĕră	tĕnĕrō		Tĕnĕrīs	tĕnĕrīs	tĕnĕrīs

Decline also (like *Bonus*) :—*Verus*, true ; *excelsus*, high ; *malus*, wicked ; *durus*, hard ; *carus*, dear ; *magnus*, great.

Decline also (like *Niger*) :—*Sacer*, sacred ; *pulcher*, beautiful.

Decline also (like *Tener*) :—*Liber*, free ; *miser*, wretched.

§ 19. Adjectives of Two Endings follow the Third Declension of Nouns : as *tristis*, sad ; *melior*, better.

1.

M. F.	N.	M. F.	N.
N. Trist-is	trist-ĕ	Trist-ĕs	trist-ĭă
G. Trist-is		Trist-ium	
D. Trist-i		Trist-ibŭs	
A. Trist-em	trist-ĕ	Trist-ĕs	trist-ĭă
V. Trist-is	trist-ĕ	Trist-ĕs	trist-ĭă
A. Trist-i		Trist-ibŭs	

2.

M. F.	N.	M. F.	N.
N. Mĕliŏr	meliŭs	Mĕliŏr-ĕs	mĕliŏr-ă
G. Mĕliŏr-is		Mĕliŏr-um	
D. Mĕliŏr-i		Mĕliŏr-ibŭs	
A. Mĕliŏr-em	mĕliŭs	Mĕliŏr-ĕs	mĕliŏr-ă
V. Mĕliŏr	mĕliŭs	Mĕliŏr-ĕs	mĕliŏr-ă
A. Mĕliŏr-ĕ *or* i		Mĕliŏr-ibŭs	

Decline also (like *Tristis*) :—*Brevis*, short ; *facilis*, easy ; *fidelis*, faithful ; *omnis*, all, every.

Decline also (like *Melior*) : *Durior*, harder ; *altior*, higher ; *pulchrior*, more beautiful.

§ 20. Adjectives of One Ending also follow the Third Declension : as *felix*, happy ; *prudens*, wise, prudent.

1.

M. F.	N.	M. F.	N.
N. Fēlix		Fēlic-ĕs	fēlic-ĭă
G. Fēlic-is		Fēlic-ium	
D. Fēlic-i		Fēlic-ibŭs	
A. Fēlic-em	fēlix	Fēlic-ĕs	fēlic-ĭă
V. Fēlix		Fēlic-ĕs	fēlic-ĭă
A. Fēlic-i *or* ĕ		Fēlic-ibŭs	

2.

M. F.	N.	M. F.	N.
N. Prūdens		Prūdent-ĕs	prūdent-ĭă
G. Prūdent-is		Prūdent-ium	
D. Prūdent-i		Prūdent-ibŭs	
A. Prūdent-em	prūdens	Prūdent-ĕs	prūdent-ĭă
V. Prūdens		Prūdent-ĕs	prūdent-ĭă
A. Prūdent-i *or* ĕ		Prūdent-ibŭs	

Decline also (like *Felix*):—*Rapax, rapacis,* rapacious ; *audax, audacis,* bold.

Decline also (like *Prudens*): *Potens, potentis,* powerful; *amans,* loving ; *sapiens,* wise.

Adjectives in *er*, of the Third Declension, have three .endings in the Nominative and Vocative Singular: as *acer, acris, acre,* sharp ; *celer, celer-is, celer-e,* swift.

1.

M.	F.	N.	M.	F.	N.
N. Acĕr	ăcr-ĭs	ăcr-ĕ	Acr-ēs	ăcr-ēs	ăcr-ĭă
G. Acr-ĭs			Acr-ĭum		
D. Acr-ī			Acr-ĭbŭs		
A. Acr-em	ăcr-em	ăcr-ĕ	Acr-ēs	ăcr-ēs	acr-ĭă
V. Acĕr	ăcr-ĭs	ăcr-ĕ	Acr-ēs	ăcr-ēs	acr-ĭă
A. Acr-ī			Acr-ĭbŭs		

2.

M.	F.	N.	M.	F.	N.
N. Cĕlĕr	cĕlĕr-ĭs	cĕlĕr-e	Cĕlĕr-ēs		cĕlĕr-ēs cĕlĕrĭă
G. Cĕlĕr-ĭs			Cĕlĕr-um		
D. Cĕlĕr-ī			Cĕlĕr-ĭbŭs		
A. Cĕlĕr-em	cĕlĕr-em	cĕlĕr-e	Cĕlĕr-ēs	cĕlĕr-ēs	cĕlĕr-ĭă
V. Cĕlĕr	cĕlĕr-ĭs	cĕlĕr-e	Cĕlĕr-ēs	cĕlĕr-ēs	cĕlĕr-ĭă
A. Cĕlĕr-ī			Cĕlĕr-ĭbŭs		

COMPARISON OF ADJECTIVES.

§ 21. Adjectives have three Degrees of Comparison—the Positive, Comparative, and Superlative.

Pos.	Comp.	Superl.
Altus, high	altior, higher	altissimus, highest.

The POSITIVE is the Adjective in its simplest form.

The COMPARATIVE is formed from the Positive by changing *i* or *is* of the Genitive Singular into *ior* (M. and F.), *ius* (N.).

The SUPERLATIVE is formed by changing *i* or *is* of the Genitive into *issim-us, a, um.*

Pos.		Comp.	Superl.
Doct-ŭs (doct-ī),	*learned,*	doct-ĭŏr,	doct-issĭmŭs
Brĕv-ĭs (brev-ĭs),	*short,*	brĕv-ĭŏr,	brĕv-issĭmŭs
Săpĭens (săpĭent-ĭs),	*wise,*	săpĭent-ĭŏr,	săpĭent-issĭmŭs
Audăx (audăc-ĭs),	*bold,*	audăc-ĭŏr,	audăc-issĭmŭs.

The Comparative is declined like *melior*, the Superlative like *bonus*.

Adjectives in *er* form the Superlative by adding *rimus* to the Nominative.

Nĭgĕr,	*black,*	nigr-ĭŏr,	nĭger-rĭmŭs
Mĭsĕr,	*wretched,*	mĭsĕr-ĭŏr,	mĭser-rĭmŭs
Acĕr,	*sharp,*	acr-ĭor,	ācer-rĭmŭs
Cĕlĕr,	*swift,*	cĕlĕr-ĭŏr,	cĕler-rĭmŭs.

The following form the Superlative in *limus* :—

Făcĭlĭs,	*easy,*	făcĭl-ĭŏr,	făcil-lĭmŭs
Diffĭcĭlĭs,	*difficult,*	diffĭcĭl-ĭŏr,	difficil-lĭmŭs
Grăcĭlĭs,	*slender,*	grăcĭl-ĭŏr,	grăcil-lĭmŭs
Hŭmĭlĭs,	*humble, low,* ·	hŭmĭl-ior,	hŭmil-lĭmŭs
Sĭmĭlĭs,	*like,*	sĭmĭl-ĭor,	sĭmil-lĭmŭs
Dissĭmĭlĭs,	*unlike,*	dissĭmĭl-ĭor,	dissĭmil-lĭmŭs.

If a vowel comes before *us* in the Nominative of an Adjective, it is compared by *magis*, more, and *maxime*, most : as,

Dŭbĭŭs,	*doubtful,*	măgĭs dŭbĭŭs,	maxĭmē dŭbĭŭs ; but,
Pĭŭs,	*godly,*	măgĭs pĭŭs,	pĭissĭmŭs.

§ 22. The following Adjectives are irregularly compared :—

Bŏnus,	*good,*	mĕlior,	optimus
Mălus,	*bad,*	pĕjor,	pessimus
Magnus,	*great,*	măjor,	maximus
Parvus,	*small,*	mĭnor,	mĭnĭmus
Multus,	*much,*	plūs,	plūrimus
Nēquam,	*worthless,*	nēquior,	nēquissimus
Dīvĕs,	*rich,*	dītior,	ditissimus
Sĕnĕx,	*old,*	sĕnior,	(nātū maximus)
Jŭvĕnis,	*young,*	jūnior,	(nātū minimus)
Extĕrus,	*outward,*	extĕrior,	extrēmus and extĭmus
Infĕrus,	*low,*	infĕrior,	infĭmus and īmus
Sŭpĕrus,	*high,*	sŭpĕrior,	suprēmus and summus
Postĕrus,	*hindward,*	postĕrior,	postrēmus and postŭmus.

§ 23. Some Comparatives and Superlatives are formed from Prepositions.

(Citrā,	*this side of*),	cĭtĕrior,	cĭtĭmus
(Intra,	*within*),	intĕrior,	intĭmus
(Ultrā,	*beyond*),	ultĕrior,	ultimus
(Prae,	*before*),	prĭor,	prĭmus
(Prŏpĕ,	*near*),	prŏpior,	proximus.

B

Compare the following adjectives :—*Dignus*, worthy ; *durus*, hard ; *altus*, high ; *integer, integra, integrum*, whole ; *latus*, broad ; *fortis*, brave ; *gravis*, weighty ; *tener, tenera, tenerum*, tender ; *felix* (gen. *felicis*), happy ; *liber, libera, liberum*, free ; *levis*, light ; *pulcher, pulchra, pulchrum*, beautiful ; *sagax* (gen. *sagacis*), sagacious ; *celeber, celebris, celebre*, famous.

NUMERALS.

§ 24. The two principal classes of Numerals are Cardinals and Ordinals. Cardinal Numerals answer the question, how many? *Septem*, seven. Ordinals answer the question, which (in point of order)? as, *Septimus*, the seventh.

§ 25. *Unus*, one ; *duo*, two ; *tres*, three ; *millia*, thousands ; and *ambo*, both, are thus declined :—

	M.	F.	N.		M.	F.	N.
N.	Un-ŭs	ŭn-ă	ŭn-um		Du-o	du-ae	du-ŏ
G.	Un-ius	ŭn-iŭs	ŭn-ius		Du-ŏrum	du-ārum	du-ŏrum
D.	Un-i	ŭn-I	ŭn-i		Du-ŏbus	du-ābus	du-ŏbus
A.	Un-um	ŭn-am	ŭn-um		Du-ŏs	du-ās	du-ŏ
A.	Un-ŏ	ŭn-ă	ŭn-ŏ		Du-ŏbus	du-ābus	du-ŏbus

	M. F.	N.	N.		M.	F.	N.
N.	Trēs	tria	Millia		Ambo	ambae	ambŏ
G.	Trium	trium	Millium		Ambŏrum	ambārum	ambŏrum
D.	Tribus	trĭbus	Millĭbus		Ambŏbus	ambābus	ambŏbus
A.	Trēs	tria	Millia		Ambŏs	ambās	ambŏ
A.	Trĭbus	trĭbus	Millĭbus		Ambŏbus	ambābus	ambŏbus

Obs.—(1) Cardinals from *quattuor* to *centum* are indeclinable.

(2) *Ducenti, ae, a ; trecenti, ae, a ;* &c., are regularly declined like the Plural of *bonus, a, um*.

(3) *Mille* is indeclinable in the Singular. The Noun following *millia* is put in the Genitive, e.g., *quattuor millia hominum*, 4,000 men.

(4) Ordinals are regularly declined like *bonus, a, um*,

No.	ROMAN NUMERALS.	CARDINALS.	ORDINALS.
1	I	ūnus, a, um	prīmus, a, um
2	II	dŭŏ, duae, dŭŏ	sĕcundus
3	III	trēs, trēs, tria	tertius
4	IV	quattuor	quartus
5	V	quinque	quintus
6	VI	sex	sextus
7	VII	septem	septimus
8	VIII	octŏ	octavus
9	IX	nŏvem	nōnus
10	X	dĕcem	dĕcĭmus
11	XI	undĕcim	undĕcĭmus
12	XII	duodĕcim	duodecimus
13	XIII	trĕdecim	tertius decimus
14	XIV	quattuordecim	quartus decimus
15	XV	quindecim	quintus decimus
16	XVI	sĕdecim	sextus decimus
17	XVII	septemdecim	septimus decimus
18	XVIII	duodeviginti	duodevicēsimus
19	XIX	undeviginti	undevicesimus
20	XX	vīginti	vicēsimus or vigēsimus
21	XXI	unus et viginti	unus et vicesimus
28	XXVIII	duodetriginta	duodetrigesimus
29	XXIX	undetriginta	undetrigesimus
30	XXX	trīginta	trigēsimus or tricēsimus
40	XL	quădrăgintā	quadrāgēsimus
50	L	quinquāgintā	quinquāgēsimus
60	LX	sexāgintā	sexagesimus
70	LXX	septuāgintā	septuagesimus
80	LXXX	octogintā	octogesimus
90	XC	nonāgintā	nonagesimus
100	C	centum	centesimus
200	CC	dŭcenti, ae, a	ducentesimus
300	CCC	trĕcenti	trecentesimus
400	CCCC	quadringenti	quadringentesimus
500	D or IↃ	quingenti	quingentesimus
600	DↃ	sexcenti	sexcentesimus
700	DCC	septingenti	septingentesimus
800	DCCC	octingenti	octingentesimus
900	DCCCC	nongenti	nongentesimus
1000	M or CIↃ	mille	millēsimus

PRONOUNS.

§ 26. Pronouns have Three Persons, 1st, the speaker, *ego*, I; 2nd, the person spoken to, *tu*, thou; 3rd, the person spoken of, *ille*, he.

§ 27. A. *Personal.*

(1) First Person.

	Singular.		Plural.	
Nom.	**Egŏ**,	*I*	**Nŏs**,	*we*
Gen.	**Mĕī**,	*of me*	**Nostrī, and nostrum**, *of us*	
Dat.	**Mīhi**,	*to*, or *for me*	**Nōbīs**,	*to*, or *for us*
Acc.	**Mē**,	*me*	**Nŏs**,	*us*
Abl.	**Mē**,	*by, with*, or *from me.*	**Nōbīs**,	*by, with*, or *from us.*

(2) Second Person.

	Singular.		Plural.	
Nom.	**Tū**,	*thou*	**Vŏs**,	*ye*
Gen.	**Tŭī**,	*of thee*	**Vestrī, and vestrum**, *of you*	
Dat.	**Tĭbi**,	*to*, or *for thee*	**Vōbīs**,	*to*, or *for you*
Acc.	**Tē**,	*thee*	**Vŏs**,	*you*
Voc.	**Tū**,	*O thou*	**Vŏs**,	*O ye*
Abl.	**Tē**,	*by, with*, or *from thee.*	**Vōbīs**,	*by, with*, or *from you.*

(3) Reflexive—Third Person.

Singular and Plural.

Nom.	(wanting)	
Gen.	**Suī**,	*of himself, herself, itself,* or *themselves*
Dat.	**Sĭbi**,	*to* or *for himself, herself, itself, themselves*
Acc.	**Sē**, or **sēsē**,	*himself, herself, itself, themselves*
Abl.	**Sē**, or **sēsē**,	*by* or *from himself, herself, itself, themselves.*

§ 28. B. *Possessive.*

Decline (like *Bonus, a, um*) :—

     Meus, mea, meum,   *my, mine*[*]

     Tuus, tua, tuum,   *thy, thine*

     Suus, sua, suum,   *his, her, its, their own.*

Decline (like *Niger, nigra, nigrum*) :—

     Noster, nostra, nostrum,   *our*

     Vester, vestra, vestrum,   *your.*

---

[*] The Vocative Masculine singular of *meus* is *mi, mi fili*, O my son.

§ 29. C. *Demonstrative* and *Determinative.*

(1) Hic, this (here).

	M.	F.	N.		M.	F.	N.
Nom.	Hic	haec	hoc		Hi	hae	haec
Gen.	Hūjus				Hōrum	hārum	hōrum
Dat.	Huic				His		
Acc.	Hunc	hanc	hoc		Hōs	hās	haec
Abl.	Hōc	hāc	hōc		His		

(2) Iste, that (there).

	M.	F.	N.		M.	F.	N.
Nom.	Istŏ	istă	istŭd		Istī	istae	istă
Gen.	Istīus				Istōrum	istārum	istōrum
Dat.	Istī				Istīs		
Acc.	Istum	istam	istŭd		Istōs	istās	istă
Abl.	Istŏ	istă	istŏ		Istīs		

(3) Ille, that (yonder).

	M.	F.	N.		M.	F.	N.
Nom.	Illŏ	illă	illŭd		Illī	illae	illă
Gen.	Illīus				Illōrum	illārum	illōrum
Dat.	Illī				Illīs		
Acc.	Illum	illam	illŭd		Illōs	illās	illă
Abl.	Illŏ	illă	illŏ		Illīs		

(4) Is, that (or he, she, it).

	M.	F.	N.		M.	F.	N.
Nom.	Is	eă	id		Ii	eae	eă
Gen.	Ejus				Eōrum	eārum	eōrum
Dat.	Ei				Iis or eis		
Acc.	Eum	eam	id		Eōs	eās	eă
Abl.	Eŏ	eă	eŏ		Iis or eis		

(5) Idem, same.

	M.	F.	N.		M.	F.	N.
Nom.	Idem	eădem	idem		Iidem	eaedem	eădem
Gen.	Ejusdem				Eōrundem	eārundem	eōrun-
Dat.	Eidem				Iisdem or eisdem		[dem
Acc.	Eundem	eandem	idem		Eōsdem	eāsdem	eădem
Abl.	Eŏdem	eădem	eŏdem		Iisdem or eisdem		

(6) Ipse, self.

	M.	F.	N.		M.	F.	N.
Nom.	Ipsŏ	ipsă	ipsum		Ipsī	ipsae	ipsă
Gen.	Ipsīus				Ipsōrum	ipsārum	ipsōrum
Dat.	Ipsī				Ipsīs		
Acc.	Ipsum	ipsam	ipsum		Ipsōs	ipsās	ipsă
Abl.	Ipsŏ	ipsă	ipsŏ		Ipsīs		

§ 30.   D. *Relative.*

Qui, who or which.

Nom.	Quī	quae	quŏd	Quī	quae	quae
Gen.	Cūjus			Quŏrum	quārum	quŏrum
Dat.	Cuī			Quĭbus, queĭs, or quĭs		
Acc.	Quem	quam	quŏd	Quŏs	quās	quae
Abl.	Quŏ	quā	quŏ	Quĭbus, queĭs, or quĭs		

§ 31.   E. *Interrogative.*

Quis?—who? which? what?

Nom.	Quĭs	quae	quĭd	Quī	quae	quae
Gen.	Cūjus			Quŏrum	quārum	quŏrum
Dat.	Cuī			Quĭbus, queĭs, or quĭs		
Acc.	Quem	quam	quĭd	Quŏs	quās	quae
Abl.	Quŏ	quā	quŏ	Quĭbus, queĭs, or quĭs		

NOTE.—When joined to a Noun *quod* is used instead of *quid*, and *qui* for *quis.*

§ 32.   F. *Indefinite.*

Decline (like *Unus, a, um*) :—

   Ullus, a, um (Genitive ullĭus), *any.*
   Nullus, a, um (Genitive nullĭus), *none.*
   Sōlus, a, um (Genitive solĭus), *alone.*
   Totus, a, um (Genitive totĭus), *whole.*
   Alĭŭs, ă, ŭd (Genitive alĭus), *another.*
   Alter, ă, um (Genitive altĕrĭus), *one of two, the other.*
   Uter, ŭtra, ŭtrum (Genitive utrĭus), *which of two.*
   Neuter, neutra, neutrum (Genitive neutrĭus), *neither.*

Decline (like *Qui*):—

   Qui-dam, quae-dam, quid-dam (quod-dam with a noun), *a certain one.*

Decline (like *Quis*) :

   Quis-que, quae-que, quid-que (quod-que with a noun) *whoever.*

Decline (like *Uter*) :—

   Uter-que, utra-que, utrum-que, *each.*

VERBS.

§ 33. Verbs have Two Voices:—1st, Active; as, *amo*, I love : 2nd, Passive ; as, *amor*, I am loved.

§ 34. A Deponent Verb is chiefly Passive in form, with an Active signification : as, *hortor*, I exhort.

§ 35. Active and Deponent Verbs are either Transitive or Intransitive.

Transitive Verbs require an object : as, *Amo Deum*, I love God ; *Sequĕre me*, follow me.

Intransitive Verbs express a state : as, *Dormit*, he sleeps ; *Morior*, I die.

§ 36. MOOD means manner. There are Four Moods: the Indicative, Subjunctive, Imperative, and Infinitive.

§ 37. TENSE means time. There are Six Tenses :— the Present, Imperfect, Perfect, Pluperfect, Future, and Future Perfect.

§ 38. In each tense there are two NUMBERS and three PERSONS.

§ 39. There are four classes, or CONJUGATIONS, of Regular verbs, known by the endings of the Infinitive Mood—āre, ēre, ĕre, īre, thus :—

1. Amāre, to love ; 2, Monēre, to advise ; 3, Regĕre, to rule ; 4, Audīre, to hear.

Before these can be learnt it is necessary to conjugate the Verb Sum.

§ 40. THE VERB *SUM*.

Sum, ĕs, fŭi, ĕssĕ, fŭtūrŭs, *to be.*

INDICATIVE MOOD.

(1) PRESENT TENSE—am.

S. 1. **Sum,**	*I am*		P. 1. **sŭmŭs,**	*we are*
2. **ĕs,**	*thou art*		2. **estĭs,**	*ye are*
3. **est,**	*he is.*		3. **sunt,**	*they are.*

(2) IMPERFECT TENSE—was.

S. 1. **Ĕram,**	*I was*		P. 1. **ĕrāmŭs,**	*we were*
2. **ĕrās,**	*thou wast*		2. **ĕrātĭs,**	*ye were*
3. **ĕrăt,**	*he was.*		3. **erant,**	*they were.*

(3) PERFECT TENSE—have.

S. 1. **Fŭi,**	*I have been*		P. 1. **fŭimus,**	*we have been*
2. **fuistĭ,**	*thou hast been*		2. **fuistĭs,**	*ye have been*
3. **fŭĭt,**	*he has been.*		3. **fŭĕrunt,**	*they have been.*

(4) PLUPERFECT TENSE—had.

S. 1. **Fŭĕram,**	*I had been*		P. 1. **fŭerămus,**	*we had been*
2. **fŭĕrās,**	*thou hadst been*		2. **fueratĭs,**	*ye had been*
3. **fŭĕrăt,**	*he had been.*		3. **fŭerant,**	*they had been.*

(5) FUTURE TENSE—shall *or* will.

S. 1. **Ero,**	*I shall be*		P. 1. **erĭmus,**	*we shall be*
2. **eris,**	*thou wilt be*		2. **eritĭs,**	*ye will be*
3. **erit,**	*he will be.*		3. **erunt,**	*they will be.*

(6) FUTURE PERFECT TENSE—shall *or* will have.

S. 1. **Fŭĕro,**	*I shall* ⎫		P. 1. **fŭĕrĭmŭs,**	*we shall* ⎫
2. **fŭĕrĭs,**	*thou wilt* ⎬ *have been*		2. **fŭĕritĭs,**	*ye will* ⎬ *have been*
3. **fŭĕrĭt,**	*he will* ⎭		3. **fŭĕrint,**	*they will* ⎭

§ 41. SUBJUNCTIVE MOOD.

(1) PRESENT TENSE—may or can.

S. 1. **Sim,**	*I may be*		P. 1. **sīmŭs,**	*we may be*
2. **sīs,**	*thou mayst be*		2. **sītĭs,**	*ye may be*
3. **sĭt,**	*he may be.*		3. **sint,**	*they may be.*

(2) IMPERFECT TENSE—might or could.

S. 1. Essem,	*I might be*	P. 1. essēmus,	*we might be*
2. essēs,	*thou mightst be*	2. essētis,	*ye might be*
3. essĕt,	*he might be.*	3. essent,	*they might be.*

(3) PERFECT TENSE—may have, should have, &c.

S. 1. Fuĕrim,	*I may*	} *have been.*	P. 1. fuĕrimŭs,	*we may*	} *have been.*
2. fuĕris,	*thou mayst*		2. fuĕritis,	*ye may*	
3. fuĕrit,	*he may*		3. fuĕrint,	*they may*	

(4) PLUPERFECT TENSE—might, would have, &c.

S. 1. Fuissem,	*I might*	} *have been.*	P. 1. fuissēmŭs,	*we might*	} *have been.*
2. fuissēs,	*thou mightst*		2. fuissētis,	*ye might*	
3. fuissĕt,	*he might*		3. fuissent,	*they might*	

IMPERATIVE MOOD.

(1). PRESENT TENSE.

S. 2. Ēs,	*be thou.*	P. 2. estĕ,	*be ye.*

(2) FUTURE TENSE.

S. 2. Estŏ,	*thou shalt be*	P. 2. estōtĕ,	*ye shall be*
3. estŏ,	*he shall be, or let him be.*	3. suntŏ,	*they shall be, or let them be.*

INFINITIVE MOOD.

PRESENT. Essĕ,	*to be*
PERFECT. Fuissĕ,	*to have been*
FUTURE. Fŭtūrus esse, or fŏrĕ,	*to be about to be.*

PARTICIPLES.

PRESENT (does not exist).	
FUTURE. Fŭtūrus, a, um;	*about to be.*

OBS.—Like Sum, are conjugated its compounds : Absum, *I am away from ;* adsum, *I am present ;* desum, *I am wanting ;* insum, *I am in ;* intersum, *I am present at ;* obsum, *I am in the way ;* praesum, *I am before, or, at the head ;* prosum, *I am serviceable ;* subsum, *I am under ;* supersum, *I am over, I am left.* Prosum takes *d* before *e* ; as, Prosum, prodes, prodest, prosumus, prodestis, prosunt.

§ 42. FIRST CONJUGATION.—ACTIVE VOICE.

Amo, ămāvī, ămātum, ămārĕ, to love.

INDICATIVE MOOD.

(1) PRESENT TENSE—am, do.

S. Ăm-o,	*I love*	P. ăm-ămŭs,	*we love*
ăm-ăs,	*thou lovest*	ăm-ătĭs,	*ye love*
ăm-ăt,	*he loves.*	ăm-ant,	*they love.*

(2) IMPERFECT TENSE—was, did, used to.

S. Ăm-ăbam,	*I was loving*	P. ăm-ăbāmŭs,	*we were loving*
ăm-ăbās,	*thou wast loving*	ăm-ăbātĭs,	*ye were loving*
ăm-ăbăt,	*he was loving.*	ăm-ăbant,	*they were loving.*

(3) PERFECT TENSE—have.

S. Ăm-āvī,	*I loved*	P. ăm-āvĭmŭs,	*we loved*
ăm-āvistī,	*thou lovedst*	ăm-āvistĭs,	*ye loved*
ăm-āvit,	*he loved.*	ăm-āvĕrunt,	*they loved.*

(4) PLUPERFECT TENSE—had.

S. Ăm-āvĕram,	*I had loved*	P. ăm-āvĕrămŭs,	*we had loved*
ăm-āvĕrās,	*thou hadst loved*	ăm-āvĕrătĭs,	*ye had loved*
ăm-āvĕrăt,	*he had loved.*	ăm-āvĕrant,	*they had loved.*

(5) FUTURE TENSE—shall or will.

S. Ăm-ābō,	*I shall love*	P. ăm-ābĭmŭs,	*we shall love*
ăm-ābĭs,	*thou wilt love*	ăm-ābĭtĭs,	*ye will love*
ăm-ābĭt,	*he will love.*	ăm-ābunt,	*they will love.*

(6) FUTURE PERFECT TENSE—shall or will have.

S. Ăm-āvĕrō,	*I shall* ⎫	P. ăm-āverĭmus,	*we shall* ⎫
ăm-āvĕris,	*thou wilt* ⎬ *have loved*	ăm-āverĭtĭs,	*ye will* ⎬ *have loved*
ăm-āverit,	*he will* ⎭	ăm-āverint,	*they will* ⎭

§ 43.   SUBJUNCTIVE MOOD.

(1) PRESENT TENSE—may or can.

S. Ăm-em,	*I may love*	P. ăm-ēmŭs,	*we may love*
ăm-ēs,	*thou mayst love*	ăm-ētĭs,	*ye may love*
ăm-ĕt,	*he may love.*	ăm-ent,	*they may love.*

(2) IMPERFECT TENSE—might, could, would, should.

S. Ăm-ărem, *I might love*
　 ăm-ărēs, *thou mightst love*
　 ăm-ărĕt, *he might love.*

P. Ăm-ărēmŭs, *we might love*
　 ăm-ărētis, *ye might love*
　 ăm-ărent, *they might love.*

(3) PERFECT TENSE—may *or* can have.

S. Ăm-ăvĕrim, *I may* ⎱ *have*
　 ăm-ăvĕris, *thou mayst* ⎰ *loved.*
　 ăm-ăvĕrit, *he may*

P. ăm-ăvĕrimus, *we may* ⎱ *have*
　 ăm-ăvĕritis, *ye may* ⎰ *loved.*
　 ăm-ăvĕrint, *they may*

(4) PLUPERFECT TENSE—might, could, would, should have.

S. Ăm-ăvissem, *I might* ⎱ *have*
　 ăm-ăvissēs, *thou mightst* ⎰ *loved.*
　 ăm-ăvissĕt, *he mightst*

P. ăm-ăvissēmus, *we might* ⎱ *have*
　 ăm-ăvissētis, *ye might* ⎰ *loved.*
　 ăm-ăvissent, *they might*

IMPERATIVE MOOD.

(1) PRESENT TENSE.

S. Am-ă, *love thou.*　　　　　P. ăm-ătĕ, *love ye.*

(2) FUTURE TENSE.

S. Ăm-ăto, *thou shalt love*
　 ăm-ătŏ, *he shall love, or, let him love.*

P. ăm-ătōtĕ, *ye shall love*
　 ăm-antŏ, *they shall love, or, let them love.*

INFINITIVE MOOD.

PRESENT. Am-ărĕ　　　*to love.*
PERFECT. ăm-ăvissĕ,　*to have loved.*
FUTURE. ăm-ăturus esse, *to be about to love.*

GERUND.

Gen. Ăm-andī,　　*of loving.*
Dat. ăm-andŏ,　　*for loving.*
Acc. ăm-andum,　*loving.*
Abl. ăm-andŏ,　　*by loving.*

SUPINES.

Am-ătum, *to love:* ăm-ătū, *to be loved.*

PARTICIPLES.

PRESENT. Am-ans, *loving.*
FUTURE. ăm-ăturŭs, a, um, *being about to love.*

§ 44. SECOND CONJUGATION.—ACTIVE VOICE.

Moneo, mŏnŭi, mŏnĭtum, mŏnērĕ—*to advise.*

INDICATIVE MOOD.

(1) PRESENT TENSE—am, do.

S. **Mŏn-eŏ,** *I advise*
  mŏn-ĕs, *thou advisest*
  mŏn-ĕt, *he advises.*

P. **mŏn-ēmŭs,** *we advise.*
  mŏn-ētĭs, *ye advise.*
  mŏn-ent, *they advise.*

(2) IMPERFECT TENSE—was, did, used to.

S. **Mŏn-ēbam,** *I was advising*
  mŏn-ēbās, *thou wast advising*
  mŏn-ēbăt, *he was advising.*

P. **mŏn-ēbāmŭs,** *we were advising*
  mŏn-ēbātĭs, *ye were advising*
  mŏn-ēbant, *they were advising.*

(3) PERFECT TENSE—have.

S. **Mŏn-uī,** *I advised.*
  mŏn-ŭistī, *thou advisedst*
  mŏn-uĭt, *he advised.*

P. **mŏn-uĭmŭs,** *we advised*
  mŏn-ŭistĭs, *ye advised*
  mŏn-ŭērunt, *they advised.*

(4) PLUPERFECT TENSE—had.

S. **Mŏn-ŭēram,** *I had advised*
  mŏn-ŭērās, *thou hadst advised*
  mŏn-ŭērăt, *he had advised.*

P. **mŏn-ŭērāmŭs,** *we had advised*
  mŏn-ŭērātĭs, *ye had advised*
  mŏn-ŭērant, *they had advised.*

(5) FUTURE TENSE—shall or will.

S. **Mŏn-ēbo,** *I shall advise*
  mŏn-ēbĭs, *thou wilt advise*
  mŏn-ēbĭt, *he will advise.*

P. **mŏn-ēbĭmŭs,** *we shall advise*
  mŏn-ēbĭtĭs, *ye will advise*
  mŏn-ēbunt, *they will advise.*

(6) FUTURE PERFECT TENSE—shall or will have.

S. **Mŏn-ŭēro,** *I shall* }
  mŏn-ŭērĭs, *thou wilt* } *have advised.*
  mŏn-ŭērĭt, *he will* }

P. **mŏn-ŭērĭmŭs,** *we shall* }
  mŏn-ŭērĭtĭs, *ye will* } *have advised.*
  mŏn-ŭērĭnt, *they will* }

§ 45. SUBJUNCTIVE MOOD.

(1) PRESENT TENSE—may or can.

S. **Mŏn-eam,** *I may advise*
  mŏn-eās, *thou mayst advise*
  mŏn-eăt, *he may advise.*

P. **mŏn-eāmŭs,** *we may advise*
  mŏn-eātĭs, *ye may advise*
  mŏn-eant, *they may advise.*

(2) IMPERFECT TENSE—might, could, would, should.

S. Mŏn-ĕrem, *I might advise*
  mŏn-ĕrēs, *thou mightst advise*
  mŏn-ĕrĕt, *he might advise.*

P. mŏn-ĕrēmŭs, *we might advise*
  mŏn-ĕrētis, *ye might advise*
  mŏn-ĕrent, *they might advise.*

(3) PERFECT TENSE—may or can have.

S. Mŏn-uĕrim, *I may*
  mŏn-uĕris, *thou mayst* } *have advised.*
  mŏn-uĕrit, *he may*

P. mŏn-uĕrimŭs, *we may*
  mŏn-uĕritis, *ye may* } *have advised.*
  mŏn-uĕrint, *they may*

(4) PLUPERFECT TENSE—might, would, could, should have.

S. Mŏn-uissem, *I might*
  mŏn-uissēs, *thou mightst* } *have advised.*
  mŏn-uissĕt, *he might*

P. mŏn-uissēmŭs, *we might*
  mŏn-uissētis, *ye might* } *have advised.*
  mŏn-uissent, *they might*

IMPERATIVE MOOD.

(1) PRESENT TENSE.

S. Mŏn-ē, *advise thou.*
P. mŏn-ētĕ, *advise ye.*

(2) FUTURE TENSE.

S. Mŏn-ēto, *thou shalt advise*
  mŏn-ēto, *he shall advise, or, let him advise.*

P. mŏn-ētōtĕ, *ye shall advise*
  mŏn-ento, *they shall advise, or, let them advise.*

INFINITIVE MOOD.

PRESENT. Mŏn-ērĕ, *to advise.*
PERFECT. mŏn-uissĕ, *to have advised.*
FUTURE. mŏn-ĭtūrus essĕ, *to be about to be advised.*

GERUND.

Gen. Mŏn-endī, *of advising.*
Dat. mŏn-endŏ, *for advising.*
Acc. mŏn-endum, *advising.*
Abl. mŏn-endŏ, *by advising.*

SUPINES.

Mŏn-ĭtum, *to advise;* mŏn-ĭtu, *to be advised.*

PARTICIPLES.

PRESENT. Mŏn-ens, *advising.*
FUTURE. mŏn-ĭtūrŭs, *about to advise.*

§ 46. THIRD CONJUGATION.—ACTIVE VOICE.

Rĕgo, rexĭ, rectum, rĕgĕrĕ—*to rule.*

INDICATIVE MOOD.

(1) PRESENT TENSE—am, do.

S. **Rĕg-o,** *I rule*
rĕg-ĭs, *thou rulest*
rĕg-ĭt, *he rules.*

P. **rĕg-ĭmŭs,** *we rule*
rĕg-ĭtĭs, *ye rule*
rĕg-unt, *they rule.*

(2) IMPERFECT TENSE—was, did, used to.

S. **Rĕg-ōbam,** *I was ruling*
rĕg-ōbās, *thou wast ruling*
rĕg-ōbăt, *he was ruling.*

P. **rĕg-ōbāmŭs,** *we were ruling*
rĕg-ōbātĭs, *ye were ruling*
rĕg-ōbant, *they were ruling.*

(3) PERFECT TENSE—have.

S. **Rex-ĭ,** *I ruled*
rex-istĭ, *thou ruledst*
rex-ĭt, *he ruled.*

P. **rex-ĭmŭs,** *we ruled*
rex-istĭs, *ye ruled*
rex-ĕrunt, *they ruled.*

(4) PLUPERFECT TENSE—had.

S. **Rex-ĕram,** *I had ruled*
rex-ĕrās, *thou hadst ruled*
rex-ĕrăt, *he had ruled.*

P. **rex-ĕrāmŭs,** *we had ruled*
rex-ĕrātĭs, *ye had ruled*
rex-ĕrant, *they had ruled.*

(5) FUTURE TENSE—shall or will.

S. **Rĕg-am,** *I shall rule*
rĕg-ēs, *thou wilt rule*
rĕg-ĕt, *he will rule.*

P. **rĕg-ēmŭs,** *we shall rule*
rĕg-ētĭs, *ye will rule*
rĕg-ent, *they will rule.*

(6) FUTURE PERFECT TENSE—shall or will have.

S. **Rex-ĕro,** *I shall*
rex-ĕrĭs, *thou wilt* } *have ruled.*
rex-ĕrĭt, *he will*

P. **rex-ĕrimŭs,** *we shall*
rex-ĕritĭs, *ye will* } *have ruled.*
rex-ĕrint, *they will*

§ 47. SUBJUNCTIVE MOOD.

(1) PRESENT TENSE—may or can.

S. **Rĕg-am,** *I may rule*
rĕg-ās, *thou mayst rule*
rĕg-ăt, *he may rule.*

P. **rĕg-āmŭs,** *we may rule*
rĕg-ātĭs, *ye may rule*
rĕg-ant, *they may rule.*

(2) IMPERFECT TENSE—might, could, would, should.

S. **Rĕg-ĕrem,** *I might rule*   P. **rĕg-ĕrēmŭs,** *we might rule*
  rĕg-ĕrēs, *thou mightst rule*   **rĕg-ĕrētĭs,** *ye might rule*
  rĕg-ĕrĕt, *he might rule.*   **rĕg-ĕrent,** *they might rule.*

(3) PERFECT TENSE—may or can have.

S. **Rex-ĕrim,** *I may* ⎱ *have ruled.*   P. **rex-ĕrĭmŭs,** *we may* ⎱ *have ruled.*
  rex-ĕrĭs, *thou mayst* ⎰   **rex-ĕrĭtĭs,** *ye may* ⎰
  rex-ĕrĭt, *he may*   **rex-ĕrint,** *they may*

(4) PLUPERFECT TENSE—might, could, would, should have.

S. **Rex-issem,** *I might* ⎱ *have ruled.*   P. **rex-issēmŭs,** *we might* ⎱ *have ruled.*
  rex-issēs, *thou mightst* ⎰   **rex-issētĭs,** *ye might* ⎰
  rex-issĕt, *he might*   **rex-issent,** *they might*

IMPERATIVE MOOD.

(1) PRESENT TENSE.

S. **Rĕg-ĕ,** *rule thou.*   P. **rĕg-ĭtĕ,** *rule yet*

(2) FUTURE TENSE.

S. **Rĕg-ĭto,** *thou shalt rule*   P. **rĕg-ĭtōtĕ,** *ye shall rule*
  rĕg-ĭto, *he shall rule, or, let him rule.*   **rĕg-unto,** *they shall rule, or, let them rule.*

INFINITIVE MOOD.

PRESENT. **Rĕg-ĕrĕ,**   *to rule.*
PERFECT. **rex-issĕ,**   *to have ruled.*
FUTURE. **rect-ūrŭs essĕ,** *to be about to rule.*

GERUND.

Gen. **Rĕg-endĭ,** *of ruling.*
Dat. **rĕg-endō,** *for ruling.*
Acc. **rĕg-endum,** *ruling.*
Abl. **rĕg-endō,** *by ruling.*

SUPINES.

Rect-um, *to rule;* **rect-ū,** *to be ruled.*

PARTICIPLES.

PRESENT. **Rĕg-ens,** *ruling.*
FUTURE. **rect-ūrŭs,** *about to rule.*

§ 48. FOURTH CONJUGATION.—ACTIVE VOICE.

Audio, audīvī, audītum, audīrĕ—to hear.

INDICATIVE MOOD.

(1) PRESENT TENSE—am, do.

S. Aud-io, *I hear*	P. aud-īmŭs, *we hear*
aud-īs, *thou hearest*	aud-ītīs, *ye hear*
audīt, *he hears.*	aud-iunt, *they hear.*

(2) IMPERFECT TENSE—was, did, used to.

S. aud-iēbam, *I was hearing*	P. aud-iēbāmŭs, *we were hearing*
aud-iēbās, *thou wast hearing*	aud-iēbātīs, *ye were hearing*
aud-iēbāt, *he was hearing.*	aud-iēbant, *they were hearing.*

(3) PERFECT TENSE—have.

S. aud-īvī, *I heard*	P. aud-īvīmŭs, *we heard*
aud-īvistī, *thou heardst*	aud-īvistīs, *ye heard*
aud-īvit, *he heard.*	aud-īvĕrunt, *they heard.*

(4) PLUPERFECT TENSE—had.

S. aud-īvĕram, *I had heard*	P. aud-īvĕrāmŭs, *we had heard*
aud-īvĕrās, *thou hadst heard*	aud-īvĕrātīs, *ye had heard*
aud-īvĕrāt, *he had heard.*	aud-īvĕrant, *they had heard.*

(5) FUTURE TENSE—shall or will.

S. aud-iam, *I shall hear*	P. aud-iēmŭs, *we shall hear*
aud-iēs, *thou wilt hear*	aud-iētīs, *ye will hear*
aud-iēt, *he will hear.*	aud-ient, *they will hear.*

(6) FUTURE PERFECT TENSE—shall or will have.

S. aud-īvĕro, *I shall* } *have heard*	P. aud-īvĕrimŭs, *we shall* } *have heard*
aud-īvĕris, *thou wilt* }	aud-īvĕritīs, *ye will* }
aud-īvĕrit, *he will* }	aud-īvĕrint, *they will* }

§ 49. SUBJUNCTIVE MOOD.

(1) PRESENT TENSE—may or can.

S. Aud-iam, *I may hear*	P. aud-iāmŭs, *we may hear*
aud-iās, *thou mayst hear*	aud-iātīs, *ye may hear*
aud-iāt, *he may hear.*	aud-iant, *they may hear.*

(2) IMPERFECT TENSE—might, could, would, should.

S. aud-Irem, *I might hear*	P. aud-Irēmūs, *we might hear*
aud-Irēs, *thou mightst hear*	aud-Irētis, *ye might hear*
aud-Irēt, *he might hear.*	aud-Irent, *they might hear.*

(3) PERFECT TENSE—may or can have.

S. aud-Ivĕrim, *I may*	⎱ *have*	P. aud-Ivĕrimūs, *we may*	⎱ *have*
aud-Ivĕris, *thou mayst*	⎰ *heard.*	aud-Ivĕritis, *ye may*	⎰ *heard.*
aud-Ivĕrit, *he may*		aud-Ivĕrint, *they may*	

(4) PLUPERFECT TENSE—might, could, would, should have.

S. aud-Ivissem, *I might*	⎱ *have*	P. aud-Ivissēmūs, *we might*	⎱ *have*
aud-Ivissēs, *thou mightst*	⎰ *heard.*	aud-Ivissētis, *ye might*	⎰ *heard.*
aud-Ivissĕt, *he might*		aud-Ivissent, *they might*	

IMPERATIVE MOOD.

(1) PRESENT TENSE.

S. Aud-I, *hear thou.*	P. aud-Itĕ, *hear ye.*

(2) FUTURE TENSE.

S. aud-Ito, *thou shalt hear*	P. aud-Itŏtĕ, *ye shall hear*
aud-Ito, *he shall hear, or, let him hear.*	aud-Iunto, *they shall hear, or, let them hear.*

INFINITIVE MOOD.

PRESENT.	Aud-Irĕ,	*to hear.*
PERFECT.	aud-Ivissĕ,	*to have heard.*
FUTURE.	aud-Itūrūs essĕ,	*to be about to hear.*

GERUND.

Gen.	Aud-iendI,	*of hearing.*
Dat.	aud-iendŏ,	*for hearing.*
Acc.	aud-iendum,	*hearing.*
Abl.	aud-iendŏ,	*by hearing.*

SUPINES.

Aud-Itum, *to hear;* aud-Itū, *to be heard.*

PARTICIPLES.

PRESENT.	Aud-iens,	*hearing.*
FUTURE.	aud-iturus,	*about to hear.*

C

§ 50. FIRST CONJUGATION.—PASSIVE VOICE.

Amŏr, amātus sum, amārī—to be loved.

INDICATIVE MOOD.

(1) PRESENT TENSE—am.

S. **Ăm-ŏr,**	*I am loved*	P. **ăm-āmŭr,**	*we are loved*
ăm-ărĭs,	*thou art loved*	**ăm-āminĭ,**	*ye are loved*
ăm-ātŭr,	*he is loved.*	**ăm-antŭr,**	*they are loved.*

(2) IMPERFECT TENSE—was being.

S. **ăm-ăbăr,**	*I was* ⎱ *being*	P. **ăm-ăbāmŭr,**	*we were* ⎱ *being*
ăm-ăbārĭs,	*thou wast* ⎰ *loved.*	**ăm-ăbāminĭ,**	*ye were* ⎰ *loved.*
ăm-ăbātŭr,	*he was*	**ăm-ăbantŭr,**	*they were*

(3) PERFECT TENSE—was, have been.

S. **ăm-ātŭs sum,**	*I was loved*	P. **ăm-ātī sŭmŭs,**	*we were loved.*
ăm-ātŭs ĕs,	*thou wast loved*	**ăm-ātī estĭs,**	*ye were loved*
ăm-ātŭs est,	*he was loved.*	**ăm-ātī sunt,**	*they were loved.*

(4) PLUPERFECT TENSE—had been.

S. **ăm-ātŭs ĕram,**	*I had* ⎱ *been*	P. **ăm-ātī ĕrāmŭs,**	*we had* ⎱ *been*
ăm-ātŭs ĕrās,	*thou hadst* ⎰ *loved.*	**ăm-ātī ĕrātĭs,**	*ye had* ⎰ *loved.*
ăm-ātŭs ĕrăt,	*he had*	**ăm-ātī ĕrant,**	*they had*

(5) FUTURE TENSE—shall or will be.

S. **ăm-ăbŏr,**	*I shall* ⎱ *be*	P. **ăm-ăbĭmŭr,**	*we shall* ⎱ *be*
ăm-ăbĕrĭs,	*thou wilt* ⎰ *loved.*	**ăm-ăbĭminĭ,**	*ye will* ⎰ *loved.*
ăm-ăbĭtŭr,	*he will*	**ăm-ăbuntŭr,**	*they will*

(6) FUTURE PERFECT TENSE—shall or will have been.

S. **ăm-ātŭs ĕrŏ,**	*I shall* ⎱ *have been*	P. **ăm-ātī ĕrĭmŭs,**	*we shall* ⎱ *have been*
ăm-ātŭs ĕrĭs,	*thou wilt* ⎰ *loved.*	**ăm-ātī ĕritĭs,**	*ye will* ⎰ *loved.*
ăm-ātŭs ĕrĭt,	*he will*	**ăm-ātī ĕrunt,**	*they will*

§ 51. SUBJUNCTIVE MOOD.

(1) PRESENT TENSE—may or can be.

S. **Ăm-ĕr,**	*I may be loved*	P. **ăm-ēmŭr,**	*we may be loved*
ăm-ērĭs,	*thou mayest be loved*	**ăm-ēminĭ,**	*ye may be loved*
ăm-ētŭr,	*he may be loved.*	**ăm-entŭr,**	*they may be loved.*

(2) IMPERFECT TENSE—might, could, would, should be.

S. ăm-ărĕr, *I might be loved*
ăm-ărĕris, *thou mightst be loved*
ăm-ărĕtŭr, *he might be loved.*

P. ăm-ărĕmŭr, *we might be loved*
ăm-ărĕminī, *ye might be loved*
ăm-ărentŭr, *they might be loved*

(3) PERFECT TENSE—may have been.

S. ăm-ātŭs sim, *I may*
ăm-ātŭs sīs, *thou mayst*
ăm-ātŭs sit, *he may*
} *have been loved.*

P. ăm-ātī sīmŭs, *we may*
ăm-ātī sītis, *ye may*
ăm-ātī sint, *they may*
} *have been loved.*

(4) PLUPERFECT TENSE—might, could, would, should have been.

S. ăm-ātŭs essem, *I might*
ăm-ātŭs essēs, { *thou mightst*
ăm-ātŭs essĕt, *he might*
} *have been loved.*

P. ăm-ātī essēmŭs, *we might*
ăm-ātī essĕtis, *ye might*
ăm-ātī essent, { *they might*
} *have been loved.*

IMPERATIVE MOOD.

(1) PRESENT TENSE.

S. Am-ărĕ, *be thou loved.* | P. am-ăminī, *be ye loved.*

(2) FUTURE TENSE.

S. am-ātŏr, *thou shalt be loved*
am-ātŏr, *he shall be loved,* or,
let him be loved.

P. am-antŏr, *they shall be loved,* or,
let them be loved.

INFINITIVE MOOD.

PRESENT. Am-ārī, *to be loved.*
PERFECT. am-ātŭs essĕ, *to have been loved.*
FUTURE. am-ātum īrī, *to be about to be loved.*

PARTICIPLES.

PERFECT. Am-ātŭs, ă, um, *loved.*
GERUNDIVE. am-andŭs, a, um, *meet to be loved.*

§ 52. SECOND CONJUGATION.—PASSIVE VOICE.

Mŏneŏr, mŏnĭtus sum, mŏnērĭ, *to be advised.*

INDICATIVE MOOD.

(1) Present Tense—am.

S. **Mŏn-eŏr,** *I am advised*
mŏn-ērĭs, *thou art advised*
mŏn-ētŭr, *he is advised.*

P. **mŏn-ēmŭr,** *we are advised*
mŏn-ēmĭnĭ, *ye are advised*
mŏn-entŭr, *they are advised.*

(2) Imperfect Tense—was being.

S. **mŏn-ēbăr,** *I was*
mŏn-ēbārĭs, *thou wast*
mŏn-ēbātŭr, *he was* } *being advised*

P. **mŏn-ēbāmŭr,** *we were*
mŏn-ēbāmĭnĭ, *ye were*
mŏn-ēbantŭr, *they were* } *being advised*

(3) Perfect Tense—was, have been.

S. **mŏn-ĭtŭs sum,** *I was advised*
mŏn-ĭtŭs ēs, *thou wast advised*
mŏn-ĭtŭs est, *he was advised.*

P. **mŏn-ĭtī sŭmŭs,** *we were advised*
mŏn-ĭtī estĭs, *ye were advised*
mŏn-ĭtī sunt, *they were advised.*

(4) Pluperfect Tense—had been.

S. **mŏn-ĭtŭs ēram,** *I had*
mŏn-ĭtŭs ērās, *thou hadst*
mŏn-ĭtŭs ērat, *he had* } *been advised.*

P. **mŏn-ĭtī ērāmŭs,** *we had*
mŏn-ĭtī ērātĭs, *ye had*
mŏn-ĭtī ērant, *they had* } *been advised.*

(5) Future Tense—shall or will be.

S. **mŏn-ēbŏr,** *I shall*
mŏn-ēbĕrĭs, *thou wilt*
mŏn-ēbĭtŭr, *he will* } *be advised.*

P. **mŏn-ēbĭmŭr,** *we shall*
mŏn-ēbĭmĭnĭ, *ye will*
mŏn-ēbuntŭr, *they will* } *be advised.*

(6) Future Perfect Tense—shall or will have been.

S. **mŏn-ĭtŭs ēro,** *I shall*
mŏn-ĭtŭs ērĭs, *thou wilt*
mŏn-ĭtŭs ērĭt, *he will* } *have been advised.*

P. **mŏn-ĭtī ērĭmŭs,** *we shall*
mŏn-ĭtī ērĭtĭs, *'ye will*
mŏn-ĭtī ērunt, *they will* } *have been advised.*

§ 53. SUBJUNCTIVE MOOD.

(1) Present Tense—may or can be.

S. **Mŏn-eăr,** *I may*
mŏn-eārĭs, *thou mayst*
mŏn-eātŭr, *he may* } *be advised.*

P. **mŏn-eāmŭr,** *we may*
mŏn-eāmĭnĭ, *ye may*
mŏn-eantŭr, *they may* } *be advised.*

(2) IMPERFECT TENSE—might, could, would, should be.

S. mŏn-ērĕr,   *I might*   } *be advised.*
   mŏn-ērērĭs, *thou mightst*   }
   mŏn-ērētŭr, *he might*   }

P. mŏn-ērēmŭr, *we might*   } *be advised.*
   mŏn-ērēmĭnĭ, *ye might*   }
   mŏn-ērentŭr, *they might*   }

(3) PERFECT TENSE—may *or* can have been.

S. mŏn-ĭtŭs sim, *I may*   } *have been advised.*
   mŏn-ĭtŭs sīs, *thou mayst*   }
   mŏn-ĭtŭs sĭt, *he may*   }

P. mŏn-ĭtī sīmŭs, *we may*   } *have been advised.*
   mŏn-ĭtī sītĭs, *ye may*   }
   mŏn-ĭtī sint, *they may*   }

(4) PLUPERFECT TENSE—might, could, would, should have been.

S. Mŏn-ĭtŭs essem, *I might*   } *have been advised.*
   mŏn-ĭtŭs essēs, } *thou mightst* }
   mŏn-ĭtŭs essĕt, *he might*   }

P. mŏnĭtī essēmŭs, *we might*   } *have been advised.*
   mŏn-ĭtī essētĭs, *ye might*   }
   mŏn-ĭtī essent, *they might* }

IMPERATIVE MOOD.

(1) PRESENT TENSE.

S. Mŏn-ĕrĕ, *be thou advised.* | P. mŏn-ĕmĭnĭ, *be ye advised.*

(2) FUTURE TENSE.

S. mŏn-ĕtŏr, *thou shalt be advised*
   mŏn-ĕtŏr, *he shall be advised,* or, *let him be advised.*

P. mŏn-entŏr, *they shall be advised, or, let them be advised.*

INFINITIVE MOOD.

PRESENT. Mŏn-ērī,   *to be advised.*
PERFECT. mŏn-ĭtŭs essĕ, *to have been advised.*
FUTURE. mŏn-ĭtum īrī, *to be about to be advised.*

PARTICIPLES.

PERFECT.   Mŏn-ĭtŭs, ă, um,   *advised.*
GERUNDIVE. mŏn-endŭs, ă, um, *meet to be advised.*

§ 54. THIRD CONJUGATION.—PASSIVE VOICE.

Rĕgŏr, rectŭs sum, rĕgi—*to be ruled.*

INDICATIVE MOOD.

(1) PRESENT TENSE—am.

S. **Rĕg-ŏr,** *I am ruled*
  rĕg-ĕrĭs, *thou art ruled*
  rĕg-ĭtŭr, *he is ruled.*

P. **rĕg-ĭmŭr,** *we are ruled*
  rĕg-ĭminĭ, *ye are ruled*
  rĕg-untŭr, *they are ruled.*

(2) IMPERFECT TENSE—was being.

S. **rĕg-ēbăr,** *I was*
  rĕg-ēbārĭs, *thou wast*
  rĕg-ēbātŭr, *he was* } *being ruled.*

P. **rĕg-ēbāmŭr,** *we were*
  rĕg-ēbāminĭ, *ye were*
  rĕg-ēbantŭr, *they were* } *being ruled.*

(3) PERFECT TENSE—was, have been.

S. **rec-tŭs sum,** *I was ruled*
  rec-tŭs ĕs, *thou wast ruled*
  rec-tŭs est, *he was ruled.*

P. **rec-tĭ sŭmŭs,** *we were ruled*
  rec-tĭ ĕstĭs, *ye were ruled*
  rec-tĭ sunt, *they were ruled.*

(4) PLUPERFECT TENSE—had been.

S. **rec-tŭs ĕram,** *I had*
  rec-tŭs ĕrās, *thou hadst*
  rec-tŭs ĕrăt, *he had* } *been ruled.*

P. **rec-tĭ ĕrāmŭs,** *we had*
  rec-tĭ ĕrātĭs, *ye had*
  rec-tĭ ĕrant, *they had* } *been ruled.*

(5) FUTURE TENSE—shall or will be.

S. **rĕg-ăr,** *I shall be ruled*
  rĕg-ērĭs, *thou wilt be ruled*
  rĕg-ētŭr, *he will be ruled.*

P. **rĕg-ēmŭr,** *we shall be ruled*
  rĕg-ēminĭ, *ye will be ruled*
  rĕg-entŭr, *they will be ruled.*

(6) FUTURE PERFECT TENSE—shall or will have been.

S. **rec-tŭs ĕro,** *I shall*
  rec-tŭs ĕrĭs, *thou wilt*
  rec-tŭs ĕrĭt, *he will* } *have been ruled.*

P. **rec-tĭ ĕrĭmŭs,** *we shall*
  rec-tĭ ĕrĭtĭs, *ye will*
  rec-tĭ ĕrunt, *they will* } *have been ruled.*

§ 55.   SUBJUNCTIVE MOOD.

(1) PRESENT TENSE—may or can be.

S. **Rĕg-ăr,** *I may be ruled*
  rĕg-ārĭs, *thou mayst be ruled*
  rĕg-ātŭr, *he may be ruled.*

P. **rĕg-āmŭr,** *we may be ruled*
  rĕg-āminĭ, *ye may be ruled*
  rĕg-antŭr, *they may be ruled.*

(2) IMPERFECT TENSE—might, could, would, should have been.

S. rĕg-ĕrĕr,	*I might be ruled*	P. rĕg-ĕrĕmŭr,	*we might be ruled*
rĕg-ĕrēris,	*thou mightst be ruled*	rĕg-ĕrĕmĭnĭ,	*ye might be ruled*
rĕg-ĕrētŭr,	*he might be ruled.*	rĕg-ĕrentŭr,	*they might be ruled.*

(3) PERFECT TENSE—may or can have been.

S. rec-tŭs sim,	*I may*	} *have been ruled.*	P. rec-tī sīmŭs,	*we may*
rec-tŭs sīs,	*thou mayst*		rec-tī sītĭs,	*ye may*
rec-tŭs sĭt,	*he may*		rec-tī sint,	*they may*

(4) PLUPERFECT TENSE—might, could, would, should have been.

S. rec-tŭs essem,	*I might*	} *have been ruled.*	P. rec-tī essēmŭs,	*we might*
rec-tŭs essēs,	{ *thou mightst*		rec-tī essētĭs,	*ye might*
rec-tŭs essĕt,	*he might*		rec-tī essent,	*they might*

IMPERATIVE MOOD.

(1) PRESENT TENSE.

S. Rĕg-ĕrĕ, *be thou ruled.*	P. rĕg-ĭmĭnĭ, *be ye ruled.*

(2) FUTURE TENSE.

S. rĕg-ĭtŏr, *thou shalt be ruled*	P. rĕg-untŏr, *they shall be ruled,*
rĕg-ĭtŏr, *he shall be ruled, or, let him be ruled.*	*or, let them be ruled.*

INFINITIVE MOOD.

PRESENT. Rĕg-ī,   *to be ruled.*
PERFECT. rec-tŭs essĕ, *to have been ruled.*
FUTURE. rec-tum īrī, *to be about to be ruled.*

PARTICIPLES.

PERFECT. Rec-tŭs, ă, um,   *ruled.*
GERUNDIVE. rĕg-endŭs, ă, um, *meet to be ruled*

§ 56. FOURTH CONJUGATION.—PASSIVE VOICE.

Audiŏr, audītŭs sum, audīrī—to be heard.

INDICATIVE MOOD.

(1) PRESENT TENSE—am.

S. Aud-iŏr, *I am heard*
aud-īrĭs, *thou art heard*
aud-ītŭr, *he is heard.*

P. aud-īmŭr, *we are heard*
aud-īmĭnĭ, *ye are heard*
aud-iuntŭr, *they are heard.*

(2) IMPERFECT TENSE—was being.

S. aud-iēbăr, *I was* ⎫
aud-iēbārĭs, *thou wast* ⎬ *being heard.*
aud-iēbātŭr, *he was* ⎭

P. aud-iēbămŭr, *we were* ⎫
aud-iēbāmĭnĭ, *ye were* ⎬ *being heard.*
aud-iēbantŭr, *they were* ⎭

(3) PERFECT TENSE—was, have been.

S. aud-ītŭs sum, *I was heard*
aud-ītŭs ĕs, *thou wast heard*
aud-ītŭs est, *he was heard.*

P. aud-ītī sŭmŭs, *we were heard*
aud-ītī estĭs, *ye were heard*
aud-ītī sunt, *they were heard.*

(4) PLUPERFECT TENSE—had been.

S. aud-ītŭs ĕram, *I had* ⎫
aud-ītŭs ĕrās, *thou hadst* ⎬ *been heard.*
aud-ītŭs ĕrăt, *he had* ⎭

P. aud-ītī ĕrāmŭs, *we had* ⎫
aud-ītī ĕrātĭs, *ye had* ⎬ *been heard.*
aud-ītī ĕrant, *they had* ⎭

(5) FUTURE TENSE—shall or will be.

S. aud-iăr, *I shall be heard*
aud-iērĭs, *thou wilt be heard*
aud-iētŭr, *he will be heard.*

P. aud-iēmŭr, *we shall be heard*
aud-iēmĭnĭ, *ye will be heard*
aud-ientŭr, *they will be heard.*

(6) FUTURE PERFECT TENSE—shall or will have been.

S. aud-ītŭs ĕro, *I shall* ⎫
aud-ītŭs ĕrĭs, *thou wilt* ⎬ *have been heard.*
aud-ītŭs ĕrĭt, *he will* ⎭

P. aud-ītī ĕrĭmŭs, *we will* ⎫
aud-ītī ĕrĭtĭs, *ye will* ⎬ *have been heard.*
aud-ītī ĕrunt, *they will* ⎭

§ 57.   SUBJUNCTIVE MOOD.

(1) PRESENT TENSE—may or can be.

S. Aud-iăr, *I may be heard*
aud-iārĭs, *thou mayst be heard*
aud-iātŭr, *he may be heard.*

P. aud-iāmŭr, *we may be heard*
aud-iāmĭnĭ, *ye may be heard*
aud-iantŭr, *they may be heard.*

(2) IMPERFECT TENSE—might, could, would, should be.

S. aud-īrĕr, *I might*
aud-īrērīs, *thou mightst* } *be heard.*
aud-īrĕtŭr, *he might*

P. aud-īrēmŭr, *we might*
aud-īrēminī, *ye might* } *be heard.*
aud-īrentŭr, *they might*

(3) PERFECT TENSE—may *or* can have been.

S. aud-ītŭs sim, *I may*
aud-ītŭs sīs, *thou mayst* } *have been heard.*
aud-ītŭs sīt, *he may*

P. aud-ītī sīmŭs, *we may*
aud-ītī sītis, *ye may* } *have been heard.*
aud-ītī sint, *they may*

(4) PLUPERFECT TENSE—might, could, would, should, have been.

S. aud-ītŭs essem, *I might*
aud-ītŭs essēs, { *thou* *mightst* } *have been heard.*
aud-ītŭs essĕt, *he might*

P. aud-ītī essēmŭs, *we might*
aud-ītī essētis, *ye might* } *have been heard.*
aud-ītī essent, *they might*

IMPERATIVE MOOD.

(1) PRESENT TENSE.

S. Aud-īrĕ, *be thou heard.* | P. aud-īminī, *be ye heard.*

(2) FUTURE TENSE.

S. aud-ītŏr, *thou shalt be heard*
aud-ītŏr, *he shall be heard, or,*
let him be heard.

P. aud-iuntŏr, *they shall be heard,*
or, let them be
heard.

INFINITIVE MOOD.

PRESENT. Aud-īrī,   *to be heard.*
PERFECT. aud-ītŭs essĕ. *to have been heard.*
FUTURE. aud-ītum īrī, *to be about to be heard.*

PARTICIPLES.

PERFECT.   Aud-ītŭs, ă, um,   *heard.*
GERUNDIVE. aud-iendŭs, a, um, *meet to be heard.*

§ 58. SIGNS OF THE TENSES AND MOODS.

Most of the Tenses may be translated in more than one way.

INDICATIVE MOOD.

PRES.   Amō, I love, am loving, or do love.
IMP.   Amābam, I loved, was loving, or used to love.
PERF.   Amāvī, I loved, or have loved.
PLUP.   Amāvĕram, I had loved.
FUT.   Amābō, I shall or will love, or be loving.
FUT.-PERF. Amāvĕrō, I shall, or will have loved.

SUBJUNCTIVE MOOD.

PRES.   Amem, I may, can, would, should, could love, or be loving.
IMP.   Amārem, I might, could, would, should love, or be loving, or have been loving.
PERF.   Amāvĕrim, I may, can, might, would, should have loved, or love.
PLUP.   Amāvissem, I might, could, would, should have loved.

§ 59. The Present Subjunctive is also used as a softened Imperative, or to express a wish.

Amem, may I love, or let me love.
Amĕt, may he love, or let him love.
Amēmŭs, may we love, or let us love.
Ament, may they love, or let them love.

§ 60. The following contracted forms of some of the Tenses are often met with :—

Amasti for ămāvisti ; ămassĕ for ămāvissĕ.
Amastĭs for amāvistĭs ; ămārunt for ămāvĕrunt.
Audĭĭt for audīvĭt ; audĭĕrunt for audīvĕrunt ; &c.

§ 61. The Third Person Plural Perfect Active often ends in ērĕ instead of ērunt, thus :—

Amāvĕrunt or ămāvĕrĕ ; mŏnuĕrunt or mŏnuĕrĕ.
Rexĕrunt or rexĕrĕ ; audīvĕrunt or audīvĕrĕ.

§ 62. In the Passive Voice we have re for ris :—

Amārĭs or ămārĕ ; ămābārĭs or ămābārĕ ; ămābĕrĭs or ămābĕrĕ.
Amĕrĭs or ămĕrĕ ; ămārērĭs or ămārērĕ ; &c.

PERIPHRASTIC CONJUGATION.

§ 63. The Participles in *rus* and *dus* may be conjugated with all the tenses of *Sum*, and this is called the PERIPHRASTIC CONJUGATION.

ACTIVE VOICE.

INDICATIVE MOOD.

PRES.	Ămātūrŭs sum,	*I am about to love.*
IMP.	Ămātūrŭs ĕram,	*I was about to love.*
PERF.	Ămātūrŭs fuĭ,	*I have been*, or, *was about to love.*
PLUP.	Ămātūrŭs fuĕram,	*I had been about to love.*
FUT.	Ămātūrŭs ĕro,	*I shall be about to love.*

SUBJUNCTIVE MOOD.

PRES.	Ămātūrŭs sim,	*I may be about to love.*
IMP.	Ămātūrŭs essem,	*I might be about to love.*
PERF.	Ămātūrŭs fuĕrim,	*I may have been about to love.*
PLUP.	Ămātūrŭs fuissem,	*I might have been about to love.*

INFINITIVE MOOD.

PRES.	Ămātūrŭs essĕ,	*to be about to love.*
PERF.	Ămātūrŭs fuissĕ,	*to have been about to love.*

PASSIVE VOICE.

INDICATIVE MOOD.

PRES.	Amandŭs sum,	*I am to be loved.*
IMP.	Amandŭs ĕram,	*I was to be loved.*
PERF.	Amandŭs fuĭ,	*I have been*, or, *was to be loved.*
PLUP.	Amandŭs fuĕram,	*I had been to be loved.*
FUT.	Amandŭs ĕro.	*I shall be to be loved.*

SUBJUNCTIVE MOOD.

PRES.	Amandŭs sim,	*I may be to be loved.*
IMP.	Amandŭs essem,	*I might be to be loved.*
PERF.	Amandŭs fuĕrim,	*I may have been to be loved.*
PLUP.	Amandŭs fuissem,	*I might have been to be loved.*

INFINITIVE MOOD.

PRES.	Amandŭs essĕ,	*to be meet to be loved.*
PERF.	Amandŭs fuissĕ,	*to have been meet to be loved.*

§ 64. FORM FOR CONJUGATING VERBS.

ACTIVE VOICE.

	1st Conj.	2nd Conj.	3rd Conj.	4th Conj.
1st Pr.Pres.	Ăm-ō	Mŏn-ĕō	Rĕg-ō	Aud-ĭō
2nd Pr.Pres.	ăm-ās	mŏn-ēs	rĕg-ĭs	aud-īs
Perfect.	ăm-āvī	mŏn-ŭī	rex-ī	aud-īvī
Pres. Infin.	ăm-ārĕ	mŏn-ēre	reg-ĕrĕ	aud-īrĕ
Ger. in di.	ăm-andī	mŏn-endī	rĕg-endī	aud-ĭendī
„ do.	ăm-andō	mŏn-endō	rĕg-endō	aud-ĭendō
„ dum.	ăm-andum	mŏn-endum	rĕg-endum	aud-ĭendum
Sup. in um.	ăm-ātum	mŏn-ĭtum	rec-tum	aud-ĭtum
„ u.	ăm-ātū	mŏn-ĭtū	rec-tū	aud-ĭtū
Part.—Pres.	ăm-ans	mŏn-ens	rĕg-ens	aud-ĭens
„ Fut.	ăm-ātūrŭs	mŏn-ĭtūrŭs	rec-tūrŭs	aud-ĭtūrŭs

PASSIVE VOICE.

	1st Conj.	2nd Conj.	3rd Conj.	4th Conj.
1st Pr.Pres.	Am-ŏr	Mŏn-ĕŏr	Rĕg-ŏr	Aud-ĭŏr
2nd Pr.Pres.	ăm-ārĭs	mŏn-ērĭs	rĕg-ĕrĭs	aud-īrĭs
Perfect.	ămātŭs sum	mŏnĭtŭs sum	rec-tŭs sum	aud-ītŭs sum
Pres. Infin.	ăm-ārī	mŏn-ērī	rĕg-ī	aud-īrī
Part. Perf.	ăm-ātŭs	mŏn-ĭtŭs	rec-tŭs	aud-ītŭs
Gerundive.	ăm-andŭs	mŏn-endŭs	rĕg-endŭs	aud-ĭendŭs

Name the principal parts of the following verbs as in the above tables:—

I.—*Laudo*, I praise; *honoro*, I honour; *judico*, I judge; *voco*, I call; *aro*, I plough; *aedifico*, I build; *creo*, I create; *canto*, I sing; *juro*, I swear.

II.—*Exerceo*, I exercise; *terreo*, I frighten; *debeo*, I owe, ought; *prohibeo*, I forbid; *mereo*, I merit, deserve.

III.—*Dico*, I say; *duco*, I lead; *jungo*, I join; *sugo*, I suck; *tcgo*, I cover.

IV.—*Punio*, I punish; *vestio*, I clothe; *nutrio*, I nourish; *finio*, I finish; *munio*, I fortify; *sepelio*, I bury; *erudio*, I educate.

IRREGULAR PERFECTS AND SUPINES.

First Conjugation.

§ 65. Most Verbs of the First Conjugation are formed regularly, like ămō, ămāvī, ămātum, ămārĕ; the following are exceptions :—

Pres.	Perf.	Sup.	Infin.	
Cŭbō,	cŭbŭi,	cŭbĭtum,	cŭbāre,	to lie down.
Dŏmo,	dŏmŭi,	dŏmĭtum,	dŏmāre,	to tame.
Sŏno,	sŏnŭi,	sŏnĭtum,	sŏnāre,	to sound.
Tŏno,	tŏnui,	tŏnĭtum,	tŏnāre,	to thunder.
Vĕto,	vĕtui,	vĕtĭtum,	vĕtāre,	to forbid.
Sĕco,	sĕcŭi,	sectum,	sĕcāre,	to cut.
Do,	dĕdi,	dătum,	dăre,	to give.
Sto,	stĕti,	stătum,	stāre,	to stand.
Jŭvo,	jŭvī,	jūtum,	juvāre,	to help.
Lăvŏ,	lăvī,	lōtum,	lavāre,	to wash.

Second Conjugation.

§ 66. Verbs of the Second Conjugation generally follow mŏnĕō, mŏnŭī, mŏnĭtum, mŏnērĕ; the following are exceptions :—

Pres.	Perf.	Sup.	Infin.	
Dĕlĕō,	dĕlēvī,	dĕlētum,	dĕlēre,	to blot out.
Flĕo,	flēvi,	flētum,	flēre,	to weep.
Dŏcĕo,	dŏcŭi,	doctum,	dŏcēre,	to teach.
Miscĕo,	miscŭi,	mistum,	miscēre,	to mix.
Tĕneo,	tĕnŭi,	tentum,	tĕnēre,	to hold.
Augeo,	auxi,	auctum,	augēre,	to increase.
Lūgeo,	luxi,	———	lūgēre,	to mourn.
Rĭdeo,	rīsi,	rīsum,	rīdēre,	to laugh.
Suădeo,	suăsi,	suāsum,	suādēre,	to advise.
Măneo,	mansi,	mansum,	mănēre,	to remain.
Jŭbĕo,	jussi,	jussum,	jŭbēre,	to command.
Haereo,	haesi,	haesum,	haerēre,	to stick.
Lūceo,	luxi,	———	lūcēre,	to shine.
Mordeo,	mŏmordi,	morsum,	mordēre,	to bite.
Pendeo,	pĕpendi,	pensum,	pendēre,	to hang.
Spondeo,	spŏpondi,	sponsum,	spondēre,	to promise.
Sĕdeo,	sēdi,	sessum,	sĕdēre,	to sit.
Vĭdeo,	vīdi,	vīsum,	vĭdēre,	to see.
Mŏveo,	mōvi,	mōtum,	mŏvēre,	to move.
Vŏveo,	vōvi,	vōtum,	vŏvēre,	to vow.

THIRD CONJUGATION.

§ 67. The parts of Verbs of the Third Conjugation are formed in many different ways.

Pres.	Perf.	Sup.	Infin.	
Rĕgŏ,	rexī,	rectum,	rĕgĕre,	to rule.
Dīco,	dixi,	dictum,	dīcĕre,	to say.
Dūco,	duxi,	ductum,	dūcĕre,	to lead.
Fīgo,	fixi,	fixum,	fīgĕre,	to fix.
Jungo,	junxi,	junctum,	jungĕre,	to join.
Tĕgo,	texi,	tectum,	tĕgĕre,	to cover.
Unguo,	unxi,	unctum,	unguĕre,	to anoint.
Trăho,	traxi,	tractum,	trăhĕre,	to draw.
Vĕho,	vexi,	vectum,	vĕhĕre,	to carry.
Vīvo,	vixi,	victum,	vīvĕre,	to live.
Flŭo,	fluxi,	fluxum,	flŭĕre,	to flow.
Strŭo,	struxi,	structum,	strŭĕre,	to pile.
Claudo,	clausi,	clausum,	claudĕre,	to shut.
Dīvĭdo,	dīvisi,	dīvisum,	dīvĭdĕre,	to divide.
Lūdo,	lūsi,	lūsum,	lūdĕre,	to play.
Vādo,	vāsi,	vāsum,	vādĕre,	to go.
Cēdo,	cessi,	cessum,	cēdĕre,	to yield.
Mitto,	misi,	missum,	mittĕre,	to send.
Nūbo,	nupsi,	nuptum,	nūbĕre,	to be married
Scrībo,	scripsi,	scriptum,	scrībĕre,	to write.
Sūmo,	sumpsi,	sumptum,	sūmĕre,	to take.
Temno,	tempsi,	temptum,	temnĕre,	to despise.
Prĕmo,	pressi,	pressum,	prĕmĕre,	to press.
Gĕro,	gessi,	gestum,	gĕrĕre,	to carry on.
Alo,	ălŭi,	altum,	alĕre,	to nourish.
Cŏlo,	cŏlŭi,	cultum,	cŏlĕre,	to till.
Pŏno,	pŏsŭi,	pŏsĭtum,	ponĕre,	to place.
Texo,	texŭi,	textum,	texĕre,	to weave.
Cerno,	crĕvi,	crētum,	cernĕre,	to discern.
Cresco,	crĕvi,	crētum,	crescĕre,	to grow.
Nosco,	nōvi,	nōtum,	noscĕre,	to know.
Pasco,	pāvi,	pastum,	pascĕre,	to feed.
Requĭesco,	requĭēvi,	——	requĭescĕre,	to rest.
Quaero,	quaesīvi,	quaesĭtum,	quaerĕre,	to seek.
Disco,	dĭdĭci,	——	discĕre,	to learn.
Curro,	cŭcurri,	cursum,	currĕre,	to run.
Fallo,	fĕfelli,	falsum,	fallĕre,	to deceive.
Cădo,	cĕcĭdi,	căsum,	cădĕre,	to fall.
Căno,	cĕcĭni,	cantum,	cănĕre,	to sing.
Caedo,	cĕcĭdi,	caesum,	caedĕre,	to kill.
Tollo,	sustŭli,	sublātum,	tollĕre,	to take up.

Crĕdo,	crĕdĭdi,	crĕdĭtum,	crĕdĕre,	*to believe.*
Vendo,	vendĭdi,	vendĭtum,	vendĕre,	*to sell.*
Vinco,	vīci,	victum,	vincĕre,	*to conquer.*
Ago,	ēgi,	actum,	ăgĕre,	*to do.*
Frango,	frēgi,	fractum,	frangĕre,	*to break.*
Lĕgo,	lēgi,	lectum,	lĕgĕre,	*to read.*
Emo,	ēmi,	emptum,	ĕmĕre,	*to buy.*
Bĭbo,	bībi,	bĭbĭtum,	bĭbĕre,	*to drink.*

FOURTH CONJUGATION.

§ 68. Most Verbs of the Fourth Conjugation are formed regularly, like audĭo, audīvi, audītum, audīrĕ; the following are exceptions :—

Pres.	Perf.	Sup.	Inf.	
Apĕrĭo,	ăperuī,	ăpertum,	aperīre,	*to open.*
Sĕpĕlĭo,	sĕpĕlīvi,	sĕpultum,	sĕpelīre,	*to bury.*
Haurĭo,	hausi,	haustum,	haurīre,	*to draw out.*
Sentĭo,	sensi,	sensum,	sentīre,	*to feel.*
Vĕnĭo,	vēni,	ventum,	vĕnīre,	*to come.*

VERBS IN IO OF THE THIRD CONJUGATION.

§ 69. Some Verbs ending in *io* are conjugated in some of their tenses like *rego*, and in others like *audio*.

Căpio, cĕpī, captum, căpĕrĕ, to take.

ACTIVE VOICE.

INDICATIVE MOOD.

(1) PRESENT TENSE.

S. Căp-io, *I take*	P. Căp-ĭmŭs, *we take*
Căp-ĭs, *thou takest*	Căp-ĭtĭs, *ye take*
Căp-ĭt, *he takes.*	Căp-iunt, *they take.*

(2) IMPERFECT TENSE.

S. Căp-iēbam, *I was taking.*	P. Căp-iēbămŭs, *we were taking.*

(3) PERFECT TENSE.

S. Cēp-ī, *I have taken.*	P. Cēp-ĭmŭs, *we have taken*

(4) PLUPERFECT TENSE.

S. Cēp-ĕram, *I had taken.*	P. Cēp-ĕrămŭs, *we had taken.*

(5) FUTURE TENSE.

S. Căp-iam, *I shall take.*	Cap-iĕmŭs, *we shall take.*

(6) FUTURE PERFECT TENSE.

S. Cēp-ĕro, *I shall have taken.*	P. Cēp-ĕrimŭs, *we shall have taken*

SUBJUNCTIVE MOOD.

(1) Present Tense.

S. Căp-iam, *I may take.* | P. Căp-iāmŭs, *we may take.*

(2) Imperfect Tense.

S Căp-ĕrem, *I might take.* | P. Căp-ĕrēmŭs, *we might take.*

(3) Perfect Tense.

S. Cēp-ĕrim, *I may have taken.* | P. Cēp-ĕrimŭs, *we may have taken.*

(4) Pluperfect Tense.

S. Cēp-issem, *I might have taken.* | P. Cēp-issēmŭs, *we might have taken.*

IMPERATIVE MOOD.

Pres. Căp-ĕ, *take thou;* căp-ītŏ, *take ye.*

Fut. Căp-ītŏ, *thou shalt take;* căp-iunto, *let them take.*

INFINITIVE MOOD.

Pres. Căp-ĕrĕ, *to take.* Perf. Cēp-issĕ, *to have taken.*

PARTICIPLES.

Pres. Căp-iens, *taking.* Fut. Cap-tūrŭs, *about to take.*

GERUNDS.

Căp-iendī, căp-iendŏ, căp-iendum.

PASSIVE VOICE.

INDICATIVE MOOD.

(1) Present Tense.

S. Căp-ĭŏr,	*I am taken*	P. Căp-ĭmŭr,	*we are taken*
Căp-ĕrĭs,	*thou art taken*	Căp-ĭmĭnĭ,	*ye are taken*
Căp-ĭtŭr,	*he is taken.*	Căp-iuntŭr,	*they are taken.*

(2) Imperfect Tense.

S. Căp-ĭēbar *I was being taken.* | P. Căp-ĭēbāmŭr, *we were being taken.*

(3) Perfect Tense.

S. Cap-tŭs sŭm, *I was taken.* | P. Cap-tī sŭmŭs, *we were taken,*

(4) Pluperfect Tense.

S. Cap-tŭs ĕram, *I had been taken.* | P. Cap-tī ĕrāmŭs, *we had been taken.*

(5) Future Tense.

S. Căp-iăr, *I shall be taken.* | P. Cap-iāmŭr, *we shall be taken.*

(6) Future Perfect Tense.

S. Cap-tŭs ĕro, *I shall have been taken.* | P. Cap-tī ĕrimŭs, *we shall have been taken.*

SUBJUNCTIVE MOOD.

(1) Present Tense.

S. **Căp-iăr**, *I may be taken.* | P. **Cap-iămŭr**, *we may be taken.*

(2) Imperfect Tense.

S. **Căp-ĕrĕr**, *I might be taken.* | P. **Căp-ĕrĕmŭr**, *we might be taken.*

(3) Perfect Tense.

S. **Cap-tŭs sim**, *I may have been taken.* | P. **Cap-tī sīmŭs**, *we may have been taken.*

(4) Pluperfect Tense.

S. **Cap-tŭs essem**, *I might have been taken.* | P. **Cap-tī essēmŭs**, *we might have been taken.*

IMPERATIVE MOOD.

Pres. **Căpĕ-rĕ**, *be thou taken;* **cap-ĭmĭnī**, *be ye taken.*

Fut. **Căp-ĭtŏr**, *thou shalt be taken;* **căp-iuntŏr**, *let them be taken.*

INFINITIVE MOOD.

Pres. **Căp-ī**, *to be taken.* Perf. **Cap-tŭs essĕ**, *to have been taken.*

PARTICIPLES.

Perf. **Cap-tŭs, ă, um**, *taken.*

Gerundive. **Căp-iendŭs, ă, um**, *meet to be taken.*

Conjugate the following Verbs like capio :—

Pres.	Perf.	Sup.	Infin.	
Făcio,	fēcī,	factum,	făcĕrĕ,	*to make.*
Jăcio,	jēcī,	jactum,	jăcĕrĕ,	*to throw.*
Fŭgio,	fūgī,	fŭgĭtum,	fŭgĕrĕ,	*to flee.*
Fŏdio,	fōdī,	fossum,	fŏdĕrĕ,	*to dig.*
Răpio,	răpuī,	raptum,	răpĕrĕ,	*to seize.*
Cŭpio,	cŭpīvī.	cŭpītum,	cŭpĕrĕ,	*to desire.*

Obs.—*Dico, duco, facio,* make *dic, duc, fac* in the Second Person Imperative Singular, *Dic mihi*, tell me ; *fac hoc*, do this.

DEPONENT VERBS.

§ 70. Deponent Verbs have a passive form, but an active meaning. They take Gerunds, Supines and Participles Active. Intransitive Deponents want the Supine in *u* and the Gerundive. *Hortor*, I exhort ; *vereor*, I fear ; *loquor*, I speak ; *partior*, I divide, conjugated like *amor, moneor, regor*, and *audior.*

D

1. Hortŏr, hortātŭs sum, hortārī, to exhort.		2. Vĕreŏr, vĕrĭtŭs sum, vĕrērī, to fear.	
INDICATIVE MOOD.		**INDICATIVE MOOD.**	
Pres.	Hort-ŏr. *I exhort.*	Vĕr-eŏr,	*I fear.*
Imp.	Hort-ābăr, *I was exhorting.*	Vĕr-ēbăr,	*I was fearing.*
Perf.	Hort-ātŭs sum, *I exhorted.*	Vĕr-ĭtŭs sum,	*I feared.*
Plup.	Hort-ātŭs ĕram, *I had exhorted.*	Vĕr-ĭtŭs ĕram,	*I had feared.*
Fut.	Hort-ābŏr, *I shall exhort.*	Vĕr-ēbŏr,	*I shall fear.*
Fut. Perf.	Hort-ātŭs ĕro, { *I shall have exhorted.*	Vĕr-ĭtŭs ĕro,	*I shall have feared.*
SUBJUNCTIVE MOOD.		**SUBJUNCTIVE MOOD.**	
Pres.	Hort-ĕr. *I may exhort.*	Vĕr-eăr,	*I may fear.*
Imp.	Hort-ărĕr, *I might exhort.*	Vĕr-ērĕr,	*I might fear.*
Perf.	Hort-ātŭs sim, { *I may have exhorted.*	Vĕr-ĭtŭs sim,	{ *I may have feared.*
Plup.	{ Hort-ātŭs essem, } *I might have exhorted.*	Vĕr-ĭtŭs essem,	{ *I might have feared.*
IMPERATIVE MOOD.		**IMPERATIVE MOOD.**	
Pres.	Hort-ārĕ, *exhort thou.*	Vĕr-ērĕ,	*fear thou.*
Fut.	Hort-ātŏr, *thou shalt exhort.*	Vĕr-ētŏr,	*thou shalt fear.*
INFINITIVE MOOD.		**INFINITIVE MOOD.**	
Pres.	Hort-ārī, *to exhort.*	Vĕr-ērī,	*to fear.*
Perf.	Hort-ātŭs esse, *to have exhorted*	Vĕr-ĭtŭs essĕ,	*to have feared.*
Fut.	{ Hort-ātūrŭs essĕ, } *to be about to exhort.*	Vĕr-ĭtūrŭs essĕ,	*to be about to fear.*
PARTICIPLES.		**PARTICIPLES.**	
Pres.	Hort-ans, *exhorting.*	Vĕr-ens,	*fearing.*
Perf.	Hort-ātŭs, *having exhorted.*	Vĕr-ĭtŭs,	*having feared.*
Fut.	Hort-ātūrŭs, *about to exhort.*	Vĕr-ĭtūrŭs,	*about to fear.*
Ger.	Hort-andŭs, *fit to be exhorted.*	Vĕr-endŭs,	*fit to be feared.*
SUPINES.		**SUPINES.**	
Hort-ātum, *to exhort.*		Vĕr-ĭtum,	*to fear.*
Hort-ātū, *to be exhorted.*		Vĕr-ĭtū,	*to be feared.*
GERUND.		**GERUND.**	
Hort-andi, *of exhorting.*		Vĕr-endi,	*of fearing.*

3. Lŏquŏr, lŏcūtŭs sum, lŏquī, to speak.

INDICATIVE MOOD.

Pres.	Lŏqu-ŏr,	*I speak.*
Imp.	Lŏqu-ēbăr,	*I was speaking*
Perf.	Lŏcū-tŭs sum,	*I spoke.*
Plup.	Lŏcū-tŭs ĕram,	*I had spoken.*
Fut.	Lŏqu-ăr,	*I shall speak.*
Fut. Perf. }	Lŏcū-tŭs ĕro,	{ *I shall have spoken.*

SUBJUNCTIVE MOOD.

Pres.	Lŏqu-ăr,	*I may speak.*
Imp.	Lŏqu-ĕrĕr,	*I might speak.*
Perf.	Lŏcū-tŭs sim,	{ *I may have spoken.*
Plup.	Lŏcū-tŭs essem,	*I might have spoken.*

IMPERATIVE MOOD.

Pres.	Lŏqu-ĕrĕ,	*speak thou.*
Fut.	Lŏqu-ĭtŏr,	*thou shalt speak.*

INFINITIVE MOOD.

Pres.	Lŏqu-ī,	*to speak.*
Perf.	Lŏcū-tŭs esse,	*to have spoken.*
Fut.	Lŏcū-tūrŭs esse,	*to be about to speak.*

PARTICIPLES.

Pres.	Lŏqu-ens,	*speaking.*
Perf.	Lŏcū-tŭs,	*having spoken.*
Fut.	Lŏcū-tūrŭs	*about to speak.*
Gen.	Lŏqu-endŭs,	*fit to be spoken.*

SUPINES.

Lŏcū-tum, *to speak.*
Lŏcū-tū, *to be spoken.*

GERUND.

Lŏqu-endi, *of speaking.*

---

4. Partĭŏr, partītŭs sum, partīrī, to divide.

INDICATIVE MOOD.

	Part-ĭŏr,	*I divide.*
	Part-ĭēbăr,	*I was dividing.*
	Part-ītŭs sum,	*I divided.*
	Part-ītŭs ĕram,	*I had divided.*
	Part-iăr,	*I shall divide.*
	Part-ītŭs ĕro,	*I shall have divided.*

SUBJUNCTIVE MOOD.

	Part-iăr,	*I may divide.*
	Part-īrĕr,	*I might divide.*
	Part-ītŭs sim,	{ *I may have divided.*
	Part-ītŭs essem,	{ *I might have divided.*

IMPERATIVE MOOD.

	Part-īrĕ,	*divide thou.*
	Part-ītŏr,	*thou shalt divide.*

INFINITIVE MOOD.

	Part-īrī,	*to divide.*
	Part-ītŭs essē,	*to have divided.*
	Part-ītūrŭs essĕ,	{ *to be about to divide.*

PARTICIPLES.

	Part-iens,	*dividing.*
	Part-ītŭs,	*having divided.*
	Part-ītūrŭs,	*about to divide.*
	Part-iendŭs,	*fit to be divided.*

SUPINES.

Part-ītum, *to divide.*
Part-ītū, *to be divided.*

GERUND.

Part-iendi, *of dividing.*

FORM OF CONJUGATION FOR DEPONENTS.

	1st Conjug.	2nd Conjug.	3rd Conjug.	4th Conjug.
1st Pers. Pres.	Hort-ŏr	Vĕr-ĕŏr	Lŏqu-ŏr	Part-ĭŏr
2nd Pers. Pres.	hort-āris	vĕr-ēris	lŏqu-ĕris	part-īris
Perfect	hort-ātŭs	vĕr-ĭtŭs	lŏcu-tŭs	part-ītŭs
	sum	sum	sum	sum
Pres. Infin.	hort-āri	vĕr-ērī	lŏqu-ī	part-īrī
Gerund in di	hort-andī	vĕr-endī	lŏqu-endī	part-ĭendī
„ do	hort-andō	vĕr-endō	lŏqu-endō	part-ĭendō
„ dum	hort-andum	vĕr-endum	lŏqu-endum	part-ĭendum
Supine in um	hort-ātum	vĕr-ĭtum	lŏcū-tum	part-ītum
„ u	hort-ātū	vĕr-ĭtū	lŏcū-tū	part-ītū
Part.—Pres.	hort-ans	vĕr-ens	lŏqu-ens	part-ĭens
„ Perf.	hort-ātŭs	vĕr-ĭtŭs	lŏcū-tŭs	part-ītŭs
„ Fut.	hort-ātūrŭs	vĕr-ĭtūrŭs	lŏcū-tūrŭs	part-ītūrŭs
Gerundive	hort-andŭs	vĕr-endŭs	lŏqu-endŭs	part-ĭendŭs

Conjugate as above the following Deponents :—

FIRST CONJUGATION.

Pres.	Perf.	Infin.	
Adūlor,	adulatus sum,	adulari,	*to flatter.*
Comitor,	comitatus sum,	comitari,	*to accompany.*
Cōnor,	conatus sum,	conari,	*to attempt.*
Contemplor,	contemplatus sum,	contemplari,	*to behold.*
Glorior,	gloriatus sum,	gloriari,	*to boast.*
Imitor,	imitatus sum,	imitari,	*to imitate.*
Interpretor,	interpretatus sum,	interpretari,	*to interpret.*
Lacrymor,	lacrymatus sum,	lacrymari,	*to weep.*
Miror,	miratus sum,	mirari,	*to wonder.*
Precor,	precatus sum,	precari,	*to pray.*
Recordor,	recordatus sum,	recordari,	*to remember.*
Vĕnĕror,	veneratus sum,	venerari,	*to reverence.*
Venor,	venatus sum,	venari,	*to hunt.*

SECOND CONJUGATION.

Pres.	Perf.	Infin.	
Confĭtĕor,	confessus sum,	confĭtĕri,	*to confess.*
Mĕreor,	mĕrĭtus sum,	mĕrēri,	*to merit.*
Mĭsĕreor,	mĭsĕrĭtus sum,*	mĭsĕrēri,	*to have pity on.*
Pollĭceor,	pollĭcĭtus sum,	pollĭcēri,	*to promise.*
Reor,	rātus sum,	rēri,	*to think.*
Tueor,	tuĭtus sum,	tuĕri,	*to protect.*

* Or mĭsertus sum.

THIRD CONJUGATION.

Pres.	Perf.	Infin.	
Fungor,	functus sum,	fungi,	*to perform.*
Ingrĕdĭor,	ingressus sum,	ingredi.	*to go into.*
Lābor,	lapsus sum,	lābi,	*to slip.*
Mŏrior,	mortuus sum,	mŏri,	*to die.*
Pātior,	passus sum,	pāti,	*to suffer.*
Quĕror,	questus sum,	quĕri,	*to complain.*
Sĕquor,	sĕcūtus sum,	sĕqui,	*to follow.*
Utor,	ūsus sum,	ūti,	*to use.*
Rĕvertor,	rĕversus sum,	rĕverti,	*to return.*
Rĕmĭniscor,	———	rĕmĭnisci,	*to remember.*
Nascor,	nātus sum,	nasci,	*to be born.*
Obliviscor,	oblītus sum,	oblivisci,	*to forget.*
Prŏfĭciscor,	prŏfectus sum,	prŏfĭcisci,	*to set out.*
Vescor,	———	vesci,	*to eat.*

FOURTH CONJUGATION.

Pres.	Perf.	Infin.	
Assentior,	assensus sum,	assentīri,	*to agree to.*
Expĕrior,	expertus sum,	experīri,	*to try.*
Mentior,	mentītus sum,	mentīri,	*to lie.*
Orior,	ortus sum,	oriri,	*to rise.*
Sortior,	sortītus sum,	sortīri,	*to take by lot.*

ADVERBS.

§ 71. There are several classes of Adverbs.   The
following are the most common :—

1. TIME.—*Nunc,* now ; *tunc,* then ; *quando,* when ! *hodie,* to-day ;
    heri, yesterday ; *cras,* to-morrow ; *jam,* now,
    presently ; *semper,* always ; *interdum,* sometimes.

2. PLACE.—*Ubi,* where ! *ibi,* there ; *prope,* near ; *huc,* hither ;
    foris, without ; *subtus,* beneath ; *unde,* whence ;
    hinc, hence.

3. MANNER.—*Bene,* well ; *male,* badly ; *fortiter,* bravely ; *sapi-
    enter,* wisely ; *sicut,* as, like.

4. DEGREE.— *Valde,* very ; *maxime,* very greatly ; *magis,* more ;
    longe, by far ; *satis,* enough.

5. AFFIRMATION.—*Certe, etiam, ita, profecto, utique,* yes, truly, &c.

6. NEGATION.—*Non, haud,* not.

§ 72. Adverbs are derived from Adjectives and Participles, and end in *e* and *ter* ; as, *ver-us* (adj.), *vere,* truly ;
liber, free (gen. *liber-i*) ; *libere,* freely ; *prudens, pru-
dentis,* prudent ; *prudenter,* prudently.

§ 73. Adverbs have three Degrees of Comparison.

The COMPARATIVE ends in *ius,* being the same as the
Neuter Singular of the Comparative Adjective (see § 21).

The SUPERLATIVE ends in *issime,* being formed from
the Superlative Adjective by changing final *us* into *e.*

Positive.		Comparative.	Superlative.
Doctē,	*learnedly,*	doctĭŭs,	doctisaĭmē
Miserā,	*wretchedly,*	mĭserĭŭs,	miserrĭmē
Prudenter,	*prudently,*	prudentĭŭs,	prudentissĭmē
Facile,	*easily,*	facilĭŭs,	facillĭmē.

§ 74. The following are irregularly compared :—

Adj.		Pos.		Comp.	Sup.
Bŏnŭs,	*good,*	bĕnĕ,	*well,*	mĕlius,	optĭmē
Mălŭs,	*bad,*	mălĕ,	*badly,*	pējus,	pessĭmē
Magnŭs,	*great,*	————	————	măgis,	maxĭmē
Multŭs,	*much,*	multum,	*much,*	plūs,	plūrĭmum.

Compare the following Adverbs :—*Alte,* highly ; *libere,* freely ; *saepe,* often ; *acriter,* keenly ; *feliciter,* happily ; *audacter,* boldly ; *pulchre,* beautifully ; *beate,* happily ; *attente,* attentively.

———————

PREPOSITIONS.

§ 75. Some Prepositions are followed by an Accusative Case alone, some by an Ablative alone, and some by an Accusative or Ablative.

The following Prepositions govern the Accusative Case :—

Ad, *to.*
Adversŭs, } *towards, against.*
Adversum, }
Antĕ, *before.*
Apŭd, *at, near.*
Circă, circum, *around.*
Circĭtĕr, *about* (of time).
Cis, citrā, *on this side.*
Contrā, *against.*
Ergā, *towards.*
Extrā, *without, beyond.*
Infrā, *below.*
Intĕr, *between.*
Intrā, *within.*

Juxtā, *near, beside.*
Ob, *on account of.*
Pĕnĕs, *in the power of.*
Pĕr, *through, by, during.*
Pŏnĕ, *behind.*
Post, *after, behind.*
Praetĕr, *beside.*
Prŏpĕ, *near.*
Proptĕr, *on account of.*
Sĕcundum, *according to.*
Suprā, *above.*
Trans, *across.*
Ultrā, *beyond.*
Versŭs, versum, *towards.*

The following govern the Ablative Case :—

A, ăb, abs, *by, from.*
Absquĕ, *without.*
Clam, *without the knowledge of.*
Cōram, *before, in the presence of.*
Cum, *with.*
Dĕ, *from, concerning.*

E, ex, *out of, from.*
Pălam, *in sight of.*
Prae, *before.*
Prŏ, *for, instead of.*
Sĭnĕ, *without.*
Tĕnŭs, *reaching to, as far as.*

The following govern the Accusative or Ablative:—

In, *into, against* (with Acc.), *in, upon, among* (with Abl.).
Sub, *up to, under* (with Acc.), *under* (with Abl.).
Subter, *under.*
Super, *over, upon.*

CONJUNCTIONS.

§ 76. Conjunctions are indeclinable words used to connect words or sentences, and show the relation existing between them.

The following is a list of some of the principal Conjunctions :—

Et, que, ac, atque, *and.*
Aut, vel, ve, *either, or.*
Nec, neque, *neither, nor.*
Sed, autem, *but.*
Nam, enim, *for.*
Ut, *that.*
Ne, *lest, that not.*

Etiam, quoque, *also.*
Si, *if.*
Nisi, *if not, unless.*
Cum, quum, *when, since.*
Quod, quia, *because.*
Ergo, itaque, igitur, *therefore.*
Dum, *whilst, until.*

INTERJECTIONS.

§ 77. Interjections are sounds used to express emotion, or to draw attention.

The most usual Interjections are :—

O, O! *oh!*
A, *ah, alas!*
Eheu, heu, hei, *alas!*

Prŏ, prŏh, *forbid it!*
Vae, *woe!*
En, eccĕ, *behold!*

IRREGULAR VERBS.

§ 78. Irregular Verbs are such as do not form all their parts according to the general rules.

1. Possum, pŏtĕs, pŏtŭī, possĕ, pŏtŭisse, pŏtens, *to be able, can.*

2. Vŏlo, vīs, vŏlŭī, vellĕ, vŏlŭissĕ, vŏlendī, vŏlendŏ, vŏlendum, vŏlens, *to be willing.*

3. Nōlo, nonvīs, nōlŭī. nollĕ, nōlŭissĕ, nōlendī, nōlendŏ, nōlendum, nōlens, *to be unwilling.*

4. Mālo, māvīs, mālŭī, mallĕ, māluissĕ, mālendī, mālendŏ, mālendum, mālens, *to wish rather.*

5. Fĕro, fers, tŭlī, ferrĕ, tŭlissĕ, lātūrŭs essĕ, fĕrendī, fĕrendŏ, fĕrendum, lātum, lātū, fĕrens, lātūrŭs, *to bear.*

6. Fīō, fīs, factŭs sum, fĭĕrī, facturŭs essĕ, factum īrī, factŭs, făcĭendŭs, *to become* or *be made.**

7. Eō, īs, īvī, īre, īvissĕ, ĭtūrŭs essĕ, ĕundī, ĕundŏ, ĕundum, ĭtum, ĭtū, ĕuns or ĭens, ĭtūrŭs, *to go.*

8. Fĕror, ferrĭs, lātŭs sum, ferrī, lātŭs essĕ, lātum īrī, lātŭs, fĕrendŭs, *to be borne.*

OBS.—1. *Fīo* is partly used as the passive of *facio.*

2. *Queo* and its compound *nequeo* are conjugated like *eo.*

3. *Noli, nolite* are used as softened Imperatives: as, *noli putare,* be unwilling to think ; *i.e.,* do not think ; *nolite judicare,* judge not ; *noli timere,* fear not.

---

* *Factum est,* it came to pass.

INDICATIVE MOOD.

Present. Possum,	pŏtĕs,	pŏtest,	possŭmŭs,	pŏtestĭs,	pŏssunt	
Vŏlo,	vīs,	vult,	vŏlŭmŭs,	vultĭs,	vŏlunt	
Nōlo,	nonvīs,	nonvult,	nōlŭmŭs,	nonvultĭs,	nōlunt	
Malo,	māvīs,	māvult,	mālŭmŭs,	māvultĭs,	mălunt	
Fĕrŏ,	fers,	fert,	fĕrĭmŭs,	fertĭs,	fĕrunt	
Fīŏ,	fīs,	fĭt,	[fīmŭs],	[fītĭs],	fīunt	
Eŏ,	īs,	ĭt,	īmŭs,	ītĭs,	ĕunt	

Imperfect. Pŏt- Vŏlē- Nōlē- Malē- Fĕrē- Fīē- I-	ĕram,	ĕrās,	ĕrăt,	ĕrāmŭs,	ĕrātĭs,	ĕrant
bam,	bās,	băt,	bāmŭs,	bātĭs,	bant	

Perfect. Pŏtŭ- Vŏlŭ- Nōlŭ- Mălŭ- Tŭl- Iv-	I,	istī,	ĭt,	ĭmŭs,	istĭs,	ĕrunt, *or* ērĕ

Pluperfect. Pŏtŭ- Vŏlŭ- Nōlŭ- Mălŭ- Tŭl- Iv-	ĕram,	ĕrās,	ĕrăt,	ĕrāmŭs,	ĕrātĭs,	ĕrant

Future. Pŏt- Vŏl- Nōl- Māl- Fĕr- Fī- I-	ĕrŏ,	ĕrĭs,	ĕrĭt,	ĕrĭmŭs,	ĕrĭtĭs,	ĕrunt
am,	ēs,	ĕt,	ēmŭs,	ētĭs,	ent	
bŏ,	bĭs,	bĭt,	bĭmŭs,	bĭtĭs,	bunt	

Future Perfect. Pŏtŭ- Vŏlŭ- Nōlŭ- Mălŭ- Tŭl- Iv-	ĕrŏ,	ĕris,	ĕrĭt,	ĕrimŭs,	ĕritĭs,	ĕrint

SUBJUNCTIVE MOOD.

PRESENT.	Poss- Vĕl- Nŏl- Māl- Fĕr-	} im,	ĭs,	ĭt,	īmŭs,	ītĭs,	int
	Fī- E-	} am,	ās,	ăt,	āmŭs,	ātĭs,	ant
IMPERFECT.	Poss- Vell- Noll- Mall- Ferr- Fĭĕr- Ir-	} em,	ēs,	ĕt,	ēmŭs,	ĕtĭs,	ent
PERFECT.	Pŏtŭ- Vŏlŭ- Nŏlŭ- Mălŭ- Tŭl- Iv-	} ĕrim,	ĕris,	ĕrĭt,	ĕrimŭs,	ĕritĭs,	ĕrint
PLUPERFECT.	Pŏtŭ- Vŏlŭ- Nŏlŭ- Mălŭ- Tŭl- Iv-	} issem,	issēs,	issĕt,	issēmŭs,	issētĭs,	issent

IMPERATIVE MOOD.

(1) PRESENT TENSE.

Sing. 2. Nōlī, *do not thou.* Fĕr, *bear thou.* Fī, *become thou.* I, *go thou.*	Plur. 2. nōlĭtĕ, *do not ye.* fertĕ, *bear ye.* fītĕ, *become ye.* ĭtĕ, *go ye.*

(2) FUTURE TENSE.

Sing. 2. Nōlītī, 3. nōlītō Fertō, fertō Itō, ītō	Plur. 2. nōlītōtĕ, 3. nōluntō fĕrtōtĕ, fĕruntō ītōtĕ, ĕuntō

DEFECTIVE VERBS.

§ 79. Defective Verbs are such as want many of the usual parts of a verb.

(1) Aĭŏ, *I say;* ăĭs, *thou sayest;* ăĭt, *he says;* aĭŭnt, *they say.*

(2) Inquam, *I say;* inquĭs, *thou sayest;* inquĭt, *he says;* inquĭmŭs, *we say.*

(3) Quaesŏ, *I entreat;* quaesŭmŭs, *we entreat.*

(4) Fārĭ, *to speak.*

(5) Coepĭ, *I have begun;* ŏdĭ, *I hate;* mĕmĭnĭ, *I remember,* are conjugated only in the Perfect and the tenses derived from it. Thus :—

Indic.	Subj.	Infin.
Coepĭ,	coepĕrim,	coepĭssĕ
Odĭ,	ŏdĕrim,	ŏdĭssĕ
Mĕmĭnĭ,	mĕmĭnĕrim,	mĕmĭnissĕ.

Imper. Sing. mĕmentŏ. Plur. mĕmentōtĕ.

(6) The Imperatives :—Apăgĕ, *begone;* Avē, *hail;* Cĕdŏ, cĕdĭtĕ, *give me;* Agĕ, ăgĭtĕ, *come;* Salvē, salvētĕ, *hail;* Vălē, vălētĕ, *farewell.*

IMPERSONAL VERBS.

§ 80. Impersonal Verbs are conjugated only in the Third Person Singular and in the Infinitive Mood.

Oportĕt, ŏportuĭt, ŏportērĕ, *it behoves.*

Dĕcĕt, dĕcuĭt, dĕcērĕ, *it becomes.*

Pĭgĕt, pĭguĭt (or pĭgĭtum est), pĭgērĕ, *it vexes.*

Pŭdĕt, pŭduĭt (or pŭdĭtum est), pŭdērĕ, *it shames.*

Paenĭtĕt, paenĭtuĭt, paenĭtērĕ, *it repents.*

Lĭbĕt, lĭbuĭt (or lĭbĭtum est), lĭbērĕ, *it pleases.*

Lĭcĕt, lĭcuĭt (or lĭcĭtum est), lĭcērĕ, *it is allowed.*

Mĭsĕrĕt, mĭsĕrĭtum est (or mĭsertum est), mĭsĕrērĕ, *it pities.*

Taedĕt, pertaesum est, taedērĕ, *it irks, disgusts, wearies.*

Ningĭt, ninxĭt, ningĕrĕ, *it snows.*

Plŭĭt, plŭĭt (or plūvĭt), pluĕrĕ, *it rains.*

Tŏnăt, tŏnuĭt, tŏnārĕ, *it thunders.*

Fulgŭrat, *it lightens.*

Gĕlat, *it freezes.*

Lūcescĭt, lūcescĕrĕ, *it becomes light.*

Vespĕrascĭt, vespĕrāvĭt, vespĕrascĕre, *it grows dark.*

The Persons are expressed thus :—

Poenitet me, *it repents me, I repent.*

So Poenitet te, eum, nos, vos, eos, *you, he, we, you, they repent.*

Poenitebit eum, *it will repent him, he will repent, &c.*

But Libet mihi, *it pleases me.*

Licet mihi, *it is lawful for me, &c.*

FIRST RULES OF SYNTAX.

§ 81. Syntax teaches how words are arranged into sentences, and how sentences are combined together.

§ 82. Syntax is divided into Concord and Government :

CONCORD treats of the agreement of words with each other in Gender, Number, and Person.

GOVERNMENT is the influence exerted upon one word by another on which it depends, in directing its Mood, Tense, or Case.

§ 83. A Simple Sentence is the complete expression of a single thought ; as—

Nox vĕnit, the night cometh.

§ 84. A Sentence consists of its Subject and Predicate.

The Subject is the person or thing about which something is said ; as—

Nox, the night.

The Predicate is that which is spoken of the Subject ; as—

Vĕnit, cometh.

§ 85. The Subject must be a Noun or some other Part of Speech equivalent to a Noun ; as—

    (a) Deus nos videt.
         God sees us.
    (b) Vos estis sal terrae.
         Ye are the salt of the earth.

§ 86. The Predicate may be a Verb, an Adjective, or another Noun ; as—

    (a) Scribae dicunt.
         The Scribes say.
    (b) Bona est lex.
         The law is good.
    (c) Spiritus est Deus.
         God is a Spirit.

OBS.—When the Verb *Sum* is used to connect the Subject and Predicate as in examples (b) and (c) above, it is called the COPULA.

§ 87. Nouns or Pronouns in Apposition are put in the same Case ; as—

> Occīdit autem Jacobum, fratrem Joannis gladio.
> *And he slew James, the brother of John, with the sword.*

CONCORD OR AGREEMENT.

§ 88. FIRST CONCORD. —A Verb agrees with its Subject or Nominative Case in Number and Person ; as—

> Non vos me elegistis ; sed ego elēgi vos.
> *Ye have not chosen Me, but I have chosen you.*

§ 89. Two or more Singular Nominatives connected by a Conjunction, generally require a Verb in the Plural ; as—

> Petrus et Joannes ascendēbant in templum.
> *Peter and John went up into the temple.*

§ 90. SECOND CONCORD.—Adjectives, Participles, and Pronouns agree with their Nouns in Gender, Number, and Case ; as—

> (a) Ego sum pastor bonus.
> *I am the Good Shepherd.*
> (b) Tu es spes mea.
> *Thou art my hope.*
> (c) Melior est canis vivens, leōne mortuo.
> *Better is a living dog than a dead lion.*
> (d) Tu es Filius meus dilectus.
> *Thou art My beloved Son.*
> (e) Vos amici mei estis.
> *Ye are My friends.*

§ 91. THIRD CONCORD.—The Relative agrees with its Antecedent in Gender, Number, and Person ; as—

> (a) Beati mortui qui in Domino moriuntur.
> *Blessed are the dead which die in the Lord.*
> (b) Sunt alia multa, quae fēcit Jesus.
> *There are many other things which Jesus did.*

THE NOMINATIVE CASE.

§ 92. The Nominative Case is used to denote the Subject of a sentence ; as—

> Creavit Deus hominem.
> *God created man.*

§ 93. The Nominative of Personal Pronouns is seldom expressed, except when emphasis is required; as—

> Quia ego vivo ; et vos vivētis.
> *Because I live, ye shall live also.*

§ 94. The Nominative is also used to describe the Subject after Verbs signifying *being, becoming, naming,* and the like; as—

(a) Omnes filii unīus vīri sumus.
We are all one man's sons.
(b) Factus es populus Domini Dei tui.
Thou art become the people of the Lord thy God.
(c) Filius Altissimi vocabitur.
He shall be called the Son of the Highest.

THE GENITIVE CASE.

§ 95. The Genitive Case generally denotes the dependence of a Noun or Pronoun upon another word, usually a Noun or Adjective; as—

(a) Ego sum panis vitae.
I am the bread of life.
(b) Et aperti sunt oculi amborum.
And the eyes of them both were opened.

§ 96. One Noun follows another in the Genitive to denote the Possessor or that from which something proceeds; as—

(a) Domini est terra.
The earth is the Lord's.
(b) Hoc est donum Dei.
This is the gift of God.

§ 97. The Genitive is used to denote the whole from which a part is taken. This is called the Partitive Genitive.

(a) Tertia pars solis, et tertia pars lunae.
The third part of the sun, and the third part of the moon.
(b) Quorum prīmus ego sum.
Of whom I am chief.
(c) Quīnque millia hominum.
Five thousand men.

§ 98. Verbs signifying *to pity, remember,* and *forget,* usually govern the Genitive; as—

(*a*) Quomodo miserētur pater filiorum.
Like as a father pitieth his children.
(*b*) Memento creatōris tui.
Remember thy Creator.
(*c*) Oblīti sunt Domini Dei sui.
They have forgotten the Lord their God.

§ 99. The five Impersonal Verbs—**misĕret**, *it pitieth;* **poenĭtet**, *it repenteth;* **pŭdet**, *it shames;* **taedet**, *it wearies;* and **pĭget**, *it vexes,* govern an Accusative of the Person, and a Genitive of the Thing; as—

(*a*) Misĕret nos hominis.
We pity the man.
(*b*) Juravit Dominus, et non poenitēbit eum.
The Lord sware, and will not repent.
(*c*) Taedet me vitae meae.
I am weary of my life.

§ 100. *Place where* is put in the Genitive if it be the name of a town and a Singular Noun of the First or Second Declension; as—

(*a*) In Ecclesiā quae erat Antiochiae.
In the Church that was at Antioch
(*b*) Cum Apollos esset Corinthi.
When Apollos was at Corinth.

In all other cases in the Ablative without a Preposition; as—

(*c*) Paulus autem cum Athenis eos exspectāret.
Now while Paul waited for them at Athens.
(*d*) Omnibus sanctis qui sunt Philippis.
To all the saints which are at Philippi.

DATIVE CASE.

§ 101. The Dative generally denotes the Person or Thing *to* or *for which* something is done; as—

Aquam pedibus meis non dĕdisti.
Thou gavest Me no water for My feet.

§ 102. Many Verbs denoting advantage or disad-
vantage, such as those of *giving, telling, pardoning,
hurting, pleasing, displeasing, persuading, believing,
commanding, obeying, resisting, envying,* and the like,
are followed by a Dative ; as—

    (a) Da mihi hanc aquam.
        Give me this water.
    (b) Hic dicet tibi quid te oporteat făcĕre.
        He shall tell thee what thou oughtest to do.
    (c) Ignoscat mihi Dominus servo tuo.
        The Lord pardon thy servant.
    (d) Leōnes non nocuĕrunt mihi.
        The lions have not hurt me.
    (e) An quaero homĭnĭbus placĕre ?
        Do I seek to please men ?
    (f) Ne forte vĭdeat Dominus, et displiceat ei.
        Lest the Lord see it, and it displease him.
    (g) Modo enim homĭnĭbus suadeo, an Deo ?
        For do I now persuade men, or God ?
    (h) Quare non crēdidi-tis ei ?
        Why did ye not believe him ?
    (i) Quia et ventis et mari imperat, et obedĭunt ei.
        *For He commandeth even the winds and water, and
          they obey Him.*
    (j) Resistite autem diabolo, et fugiet a vobis.
        Resist the devil, and he will flee from you.
    (k) Invidēbant ei igitur fratres sui.
        And his brethren envied him.

§ 103. The compounds of **sum** (except **possum**) are
followed by a Dative Case ; as—

    (a) Unum tĭbi deest.
        One thing thou lackest.
    (b) Quid enim proderit homĭni ?
        For what shall it profit a man ?

§ 104. **Est** and **sunt** with a Dative often imply
having ; as—

    (a) Non sunt nobis plus quam quinque panes.
        We have no more but five loaves.
    (b) Quod tibi nomen est ?
        What is thy name ?
    (c) Legio mihi nomen est.
        My name is Legion.

E

§ 105. The Impersonal Verbs licet, *it is lawful;* libet, *it pleases;* and expedit, *it is expedient,* govern the Dative; as—

    (a) Non licet tibi habēre uxōrem fratris tui.
       It is not lawful for thee to have thy brother's wife.
    (b) Expedit vobis ut ego vadam.
       It is expedient for you that I go away.

ACCUSATIVE CASE.

§ 106. The Accusative denotes the direct object of an action.

§ 107. Transitive Verbs, whether Active or Deponent, generally govern an Accusative Case; as—

    (a) Deus coelum et terram creavit.
       God created the heaven and the earth.
    (b) Magister, sequar te.
       Master, I will follow Thee.

§ 108. Many Prepositions govern the Accusative Case. (See § 75.)

§ 109. Four Prepositions govern the Accusative when they denote motion. (See § 75.)

§ 110. Time, *how long,* is put in the Accusative; as—

       Et mansit ibi duos dies.
       And he abode there two days.

§ 111. Names of towns and small islands, with domum, *home,* and rus, *to the country,* are put in the Accusative without Prepositions after Verbs signifying *motion towards;* as—

    (a) Ecce ascendīmus Jerosolymam.
       Behold, we go up to Jerusalem.
    (b) Vēni mecum domum.
       Come home with me.

§ 112. The Accusative is also used after many Prepositions signifying *motion towards;* as—

> Vadit ad monumentum, ut ploret ibi.
> *She goeth to the grave to weep there.*

§ 113. Verbs of *saying, knowing,* and *declaring* are followed by an Accusative with the Infinitive; as—

> (*a*) Quem dicunt homines esse Filium hominis ?
> *Whom do men say that I the Son of Man am ?*
> (*b*) Vos autem quem me esse dicĭtis ?
> *But whom say ye that I am ?*

VOCATIVE CASE.

§ 114. The Vocative is used in addressing others.

· § 115. The Vocative may be used with or without an Interjection; as—

> (*a*) O mucro Domini !
> *O thou sword of the Lord !*
> (*b*) Audīte filii, disciplīnam patris.
> *Hear, ye children, the instruction of a father.*

ABLATIVE CASE.

§ 116. The Ablative denotes the Cause, Manner, Means, Instrument, Time, Place, and Accompanying Circumstances.

§ 117. The *thing with which* is expressed by an Ablative without a Preposition; as—

> (*a*) Lapidabunt te lapĭdĭbus.
> *They shall stone thee with stones.*
> (*b*) Juda, osculo Filium hominis tradis ?
> *Judas, betrayest thou the Son of Man with a kiss ?*

§ 118. The *Person by whom* is expressed by an Ablative with the Preposition *a* or *ab* ; as—

> Agebatur a Spiritu in desertum.
> *He was led by the Spirit into the wilderness.*

§ 119. *Place where* is expressed by an Ablative ; as—

> In domo Patris mei mansiones multae sunt.
> *In my Father's house are many mansions.*

§ 120. *Time when* is expressed by an Ablative without a Preposition ; as—

Mense secundo, septimo et vigesimo die mensis.
In the second month, on the seven-and-twentieth day of the month.

§ 121. *Price* is put in the Ablative ; as—

Vendiderunt eum Ismaelitis viginti argenteis.
They sold him to the Ishmaelites for twenty pieces of silver.

§ 122. **Fungor, fruor, utor, vescor**, govern an Ablative ; as—

> (a) Cum sacerdotio fungeretur.
> *When he executed the priest's office.*
> (b) Ut fruatur parte sua.
> *That he may enjoy his portion.*
> (c) Modico vino utere.
> *Use a little wine.*
> (d) Nisi panem quo vescebatur.
> *Save the bread which he did eat.*

§ 123. Verbs or Adjectives denoting *fulness* or *want*, often govern an Ablative ; as—

> (a) Esurientes implevit bonis.
> *He hath filled the hungry with good things.*
> (b) Non egebunt lumine lucernae, neque lumine solis.
> *They (shall) need no candle, neither light of the sun.*
> (c) Musto pleni sunt isti.
> *These men are full of new wine.*

§ 124. The Adjectives **dignus**, *worthy*, and **contentus**, *contented*, govern an Ablative ; as—

> (a) Dignus est operarius mercede sua.
> *The labourer is worthy of his reward.*

(*b*) Contenti estote stipendiis vestris.
Be content with your wages.

§ 125. The *thing compared* is put in the Ablative after an Adjective in the Comparative Degree; as—

(*a*) Non est servus major domino suo.
The servant is not greater than his lord.

But when the Comparative is followed by *quam*, the objects compared are put in the same case; as—

(*b*) Neque enim melior sum quam patres mei.
For I am not better than my fathers.

§ 126. The Ablative Absolute is a clause put in the Ablative Case to express time and accompanying circumstances, and consists of a Noun or Pronoun, and an Adjective or Participle in agreement; as—

(*a*) Acce tis autem quinque panibus, et duobus piscibus.
Then He took the five loaves and the two fishes.
(*b*) Navigantibus illis, obdormivit.
As they sailed, He fell asleep.

§ 127. Many Prepositions govern the Ablative. (See § 75.)

———

ADJECTIVES.

§ 128. Adjectives are often used without Nouns in the Masculine Gender to denote Persons, and in the Neuter Gender to denote Things; as—

(*a*) Omnes scient me.
All shall know me.
(*b*) Bene omnia fēcit.
He hath done all things well.
(*c*) Omnia mea tua sunt.
All that I have is thine.

VERBS.

1. INDICATIVE MOOD.

§ 129. The Indicative states as a fact, or asks a question; as—

    (a) Lacrymatus est Jesus.
    Jesus wept.
    (b) Ubi posuistis eum?
    Where have ye laid him?

§ 130. The Present Tense is used of that which *is* now taking place; as—

    Ecce somniator vĕnit.
    Behold the dreamer cometh.

§ 131. The Imperfect Tense is used of that which *was* going on at the time named, or was wont to be done; as—

    Edēbant, et bibēbant; emēbant et vendēbant.
    They did eat, they drank; they bought, they sold.

§ 132. The Perfect Tense speaks of a past action; as—

    Quis me tŏtĭgĭt?
    Who touched me?

§ 133. The Pluperfect Tense shows that something *had* taken place at the time spoken of; as—

    In quo posuit hominem quem formaverat.
    And there He put the man whom He had formed.

§ 134. The Future Tense shows that something *will* take place in time to come; as—

    Resurget frater tuus.
    Thy brother shall rise again.

§ 135. The Future Perfect Tense is used of that which *will have* taken place by the time named; as—

    (a) Cum vēnerit Filius hominis in majestate suā.
    When the Son of Man shall (have) come in His glory.

The Future Perfect is sometimes translated by an English present; as—

> (b) Si ascendero in coelum, tu illic es.
> *If I ascend up into heaven Thou art there.*

2. SUBJUNCTIVE MOOD.

§ 136. The Subjunctive Mood represents a state or action not as a fact, like the Indicative, but merely as a conception of the mind. Hence, it is used to indicate a supposition, doubt or uncertainty, a wish or purpose, a possibility, and even a permission; as—

(a) Si quo minus, dixissem vobis.
If it were not so, I would have told you.
(b) Sustulērunt lapides Judaei, ut lapidārent eum.
Then the Jews took up stones to stone Him.
(c) Cogitabat qualis esset ista salutatio.
She cast in her mind what manner of salutation this should be.

§ 137. The Subjunctive Present is often used as an Imperative, and takes ne for *not;* as—

> (a) Manducēmus et bibāmus.
> *Let us eat and drink.*
> (b) Ne timeas, Zacharia.
> *Fear not, Zacharias.*
> (c) Tollat crucem suam, et sequātur me.
> *Let him take up his cross and follow Me.*

3. IMPERATIVE MOOD.

§ 138. The Imperative Mood commands or entreats; as—

> (a) Tollĭte lapidem.
> *Take away the stone.*
> (b) Laudāte Dominum.
> *Praise ye the Lord.*

4. INFINITIVE MOOD.

§ 139. When two Verbs come together the latter is found in the Infinitive Mood; as—

> Solvĭte eum, et sĭnĭte abīre.
> *Loose him, and let him go.*

PARTICIPLES.

§ 140. Active Participles govern the same Case as the Verb to which they belong ; as—

(a) Et reversi sunt pastōres glorificantes et laudantes Deum.
   And the shepherds returned, glorifying and praising God.
(b) Credens omnibus quae in lĕge et prophetis scripta sunt.
   Believing all things which are written in the law and the prophets.

§ 141. Participles are often construed by Verbs ; as—

   Et surgens, vēnit ad patrem suum.
   And he arose, and came to his father.

§ 142. Participles may be construed by Verbs with " when " ; as—

   Ingressus in templum Domini.
   When he went into the temple of the Lord.

THE VULGATE LATIN COURSE.

Part II.—DELECTUS.

"Quaesivit verba utilia."—ECCLES. XII., 10.

m.	masculine.	*conj.*	conjunction.
f.	feminine.	*interj.*	interjection.
n.	neuter.	*comp. adj.*	adjective in the comparative degree.
c.	common.		
pl.	plural.	*sup. adj.*	adjective in the superlative degree.
adv.	adverb.		
prep.	preposition.	*num. adj.*	numeral adjective.

OBS.—The numerals after the Nouns and Verbs show to what Declension and Conjugation they belong. The Genitive endings of the Nouns, and the Nominative Singular in each Gender of the Pronouns and Adjectives are given, together with the principal parts of the Verbs ; § refers to the Grammar, where the forms are given in full. The meanings of the words given in the vocabularies are those appropriate to the exercise, and are not always the most usual and general significations.

EXERCISE I.

Agreement of the Adjective with its Noun. §§ 1—20, and 90.

Alt-us, a, um, *high.*
bon-us, a, um, *good.*
brěv-is, e, *short.*
dilect-us, a, um, *beloved.*
fīlǐ-us, i, 2, *m., a son.*
frāter, fratris, 3, *m., a brother.*
homo, hŏmǐn-is, 3, *m., a man.*
labor, labōr-is, 3, *m., labour.*
lex, lěg-is, 3, *f., a law.*
măl-us, a, um, *bad.*
māter, matr-is, 3, *f., a mother.*
mendax, mendāc-is, *deceitful.*

mūr-us, i, 2, *m., a wall.*
nŏmen, nomǐn-is, 3, *n., a name.*
omn-is, e, *all.*
pastor, pastŏr-is, 3, *m., a shepherd.*
pater, patr-is, 3, *m., a father.*
pŏtens, pŏtent-is, *powerful.*
săcer, sacr-a, sacr-um, *sacred.*
sapiens, sapient-is, *wise.*
stult-us, a, um, *foolish.*
templ-um, i, 2, *n., a temple.*
vīn-um, i, 2, *n., wine.*
vir, viri, *m., a man.* § 16.

vǐt-a, ae, 1, *f., life.*

1. Pater bonus. 2. Mater bona. 3. Bonum vinum.
4. Bonus frater. 5. Vita brevis. 6. Vir bonus. 7. Frater
malus. 8. Nomen bonum. 9. Vir mendax. 10. Filius
sapiens. 11. Viri potentes. 12. Pueri stulti. 13. Stultus
homo. 14. Omnis labor.

15. Templum sacrum. 16. Alti muri. 17. Pastor
bonus. 18. Filius dilectus. 19. Bona lex. 20. Breves
leges. 21. Pastores mali. 22. Omne templum. 23. Boni
homines. 24. Stulti pastores. 25. Omnia nomina. 26.
Lex brevis. 27. Omnia templa sacra. 28. Omnes boni
pastores. 29. Omnes bonae matres.

EXERCISE II.

Agreement of the Adjective with its Noun—continued.

Alb-us, a, um, *white.*
angel-us, i, 2, *m., an angel.*
ănĭmal, animāl-is, 3, *n., an animal.*
ăqu-a, ae, 1, *f., water.*
ĕpistŏl-a, ae, 1, *f., a letter.*
equ-us, i, 2, *m., a horse.*
excels-us, a, um, *high.*
fīli-a, ae, 1, *f., a daughter.*
fort-is, e, *brave.*
lĭber, lĭbr-i, 2, *m., a book.*
lŏc-us, i, 2, *m., a place.*
long-us, a, um, *long.*
magn-us, a, um, *great, large.*
mendax, mendāc-is, *false.*
mens-a, ae, 1, *f., a table.*

mīles, mīlĭt-is, 3, *m., a soldier.*
mons, mont-is, 3, *m., a mountain.*
mŭlier, mŭlĭĕr-is, 3, *f., a woman.*
mult-us, a, um, *much, many.*
niger, nigr-a, nigr-um, *black.*
ŏcŭl-us, i, 2, *m., an eye.*
ŏpŭs, ŏpĕr-is, 3, *n., a work.*
parv-us, a, um, *small.*
prŏfund-us, a, um, *deep.*
puell-a, ae, 1, *f., a girl.*
puer, puer-i, 2, *m., a boy.*
pur-us, a, um, *pure.*
rex, rēg-is, 3, *m., a king.*
tempus, tempŏr-is, 3, *n., time.*
test-is, test-is, 3, *c., a witness.*

via, viae, 1, *f., a way.*

1. Epistola longa. 2. Boni libri. 3. Magnus liber. 4.
Multa animalia. 5. Mensa longa. 6. Murus longus. 7.
Parva puella. 8. Puellae bonae. 9. Mare profundum.
10. Bonum opus. 11. Magnum opus. 12. Montes excelsi.
13. Equus albus. 14. Equi nigri. 15. Pueri sapientes.
16. Omnis oculus.

17. Omnis locus. 18. Aqua profunda. 19. Bona mulier.
20. Omnes angeli. 21. Tempus breve. 22. Testis mendax.
23. Aqua pura. 24. Multi nigri equi. 25. Reges potentes.
26. Filia bona. 27. Via longa. 28. Miles fortis. 29.
Omnes milites fortes. 30. Omnes bonae mulieres. 31.
Omnis filia bona. 32. Omnia bona opera.

EXERCISE III.

Comparison of Adjectives. §§ 21—23.

Arbor, arbŏr-is, 3, *f.*, *a tree.*
bell-um, i, 2, *n.*, *war.*
difficil-is, e, *difficult.*
doct-us, a, um, *learned.*
făcil-is, e, *easy.*
infelix, infelic-is, *unhappy.*

miser, miser-a, miser-um, *wretched.*
optim-us, a, um, sup. adj., *best.* § 22.
pessim-us, a, um, sup. adj., *worst.* § 22
pŏpŭl-us, i, 2, *m.*, *people.*
pulcher, chra, chrum, *beautiful.*
ŭtil-is, e, *useful.*

1. Mons altissimus.[1]   2. Vir doctissimus.   3. Bellum longum.   4. Equi nigriores.   5. Equus utilior.   6. Mater infelicior.   7. Homines doctiores.   8. Murus altior.   9. Pueri sapientiores.   10. Labores facillimi.   11. Via facillima.   12. Equi nigerrimi.   13. Optima puella.   14. Optimi pueri.

15. Viri potentiores.   16. Populus potentissimus.   17. Mulieres miserrimae.   18. Via longissima.   19. Miles fortissimus.   20. Pueri pessimi.   21. Arbores altissimae. 22. Murus longissimus.   23. Mensae longiores.   24. Via brevior.   25. Pulcherrima animalia.   26. Opus difficillimum. 27. Multa opera difficillima.   28. Omnes optimae puellae. 29. Omnes montes altissimi.

[1] *Mons altissimus* may be translated, the highest mountain, or, a very high mountain ; *vir doctissimus,* the most learned man, or, a very learned man.

EXERCISE IV.

Numerals. §§ 24, 25.

Corn-us, ûs, 4, *n.*, *a horn.*
corpus, corpŏr-is, 3, *n.*, *a body.*
dies, diēi, 5, *m.* or *f.*, *a day.* § 15.
dŭo, dŭ-ae, dŭ-o, *two.*
hort-us, i, 2, *m.*, *a garden.*
măgister, măgistr-i, 2, *m.*, *a master.*
nox, noct-is, 3, *f.*, *night.*
pars, part-is, 3, *f.*, *a part.*

ros-a, ae, 1, *f.*, *a rose.*
scrib-a, ae, 1, *m.*, *a scribe.*
septem, *seven.*
spirit-us, ûs, 4, *m.*, *a spirit.*
stell-a, ae, 1, *f.*, *a star.*
trēs, tria, *three.* § 25.
un-us, a, um, *one.* § 25.

1. Unus magister.   2. Una nox.   3. Unum nomen. 4. Duo dies.   5. Duae matres.   6. Duo cornua.   7. Tres dentes.   8. Tres partes.   9. Tria corpora.   10. Trecenti horti.   11. Sexcentae rosae.   12. Quadringenta templa. 13. Septem spiritûs.   14. Septem stellae.

15. Quattuor animalia. 16. Quattuor angeli. 17. Tertium animal. 18. Primus angelus. 19. Secundus angelus. 20. Tertia pars. 21. Dies tres. 22. Quinque millia. 23. Primus homo. 24. Decem pueri. 25. Una mensa. 26. Secunda puella. 27. Dies sextus. 28. Unus scriba.

EXERCISE V.
Pronouns. §§ *26—32.*

Ali-us, a, ud, *another.* § 32.
amic-us, i, 2, *m., a friend.*
Dĕus, Dei, *God.* § 16.
dŏmus, ûs, *f., a house.* § 16.
dōn-um, i, 2, *n., a gift.*
gens, gent-is, 3, *f., people.*
hic, hæc, hoc, *this.* § 29.
ille, illa, illud, *that.* § 29.
iste, ista, istud, *that.* § 29.
me-us, a, um, *my.* § 28.
mund-us, i, 2, *m., the world.*
noster, nostr-a, nostr-um, *our.* § 28.
praemi-um, i, 2, *n., reward.*

quidam, quaedam, quoddam, *a certain.* § 32.
sign-um, 2, *n., a sign.*
spes, spĕi, 5, *f., hope.*
su-us, a, um, *his, hers, its.* § 28.
tot-us, a, um, *the whole.* § 32.
tu-us, a, um, *thy.*
urbs, urb-is, 3, *f., a city.*
uterque, utraque, utrumque, *each.*
verb-um, i, 2, *n., a word.*
vester, vestr-a, vestr-um, *your.* § 28.
vox, vŏc-is, 3, *f., a voice.*

1. Pater meus. 2. Pater noster bonus. 3. Mater mea. 4. Mater tua bona. 5. Liber meus. 6. Pater vester. 7. Magister noster. 8. Mater nostra. 9. Vox sua. 10. Corpus suum. 11. Praemium tuum. 12. Hic labor. 13. Hoc opus. 14. Corpus meum. 15. Haec verba. 16. Hoc signum.

17. Opera tua. 18. Labor vester. 19. Fratres mei. 20. Hoc donum. 21. Deus meus. 22. Spes mea. 23. Amici mei. 24. Isti homines. 25. Alius angelus. 26. Domus mea. 27. Quidam homo. 28. Quaedam mulieres. 29. Epistola mea longa. 30. Filia nostra parva. 31. Illud vinum bonum.

32. Haec mala mulier. 33. Hic amicus bonus. 34. Hi homines fortes. 35. Haec gens. 36. Donum meum. 37. Hi omnes. 38. Hoc praemium. 39. Hae leges. 40. Hi montes excelsi. 41. Hi montes altissimi. 42. Mundus totus. 43. Utraque puella. 44. Tota urbs. 45. Omne verbum. 46. Quidam vir. 47. Omnia mea tua sunt.[1]

[1] See § 128 (c), literally, *all my (things) are thy (things).*

EXERCISE VI.

The Genitive Case. §§ 95—97.

Agn-us, i, 2, *m., a lamb.*
călor, călŏr-is, 3, *m., heat.*
Christ-us, i, 2, *m., Christ.*
cŏrŏn-a, ae, 1, *f., a crown.*
crĕător, ŏris, 3, *m., the creator.*
curr-us, ûs, 4, *m., a chariot.*
Dŏmĭn-us, 1, 2, *m., the Lord.*
grex, grĕg-is, 3, *m., a flock.*
ĭnĭti-um, 1, 2, *n., a beginning.*
Judae-i, orum, 2, *m. pl., the Jews.*
lun-a, ae, 1, *f., the moon.*
lux, luc-is, 3, *f., light.*
măn-us, ûs, 4, *f., a hand.*
mucr-o, ŏnis, 3, *m., a sword.*

ŏvis, ŏvis, 3, *f., a sheep.*
păn-is, păn-is, 3, *m., bread.*
parens, parent-is, 3, *c., a parent.*
port-a, ae, 1, *f., a gate.*
prim-us, a, um, *first, chief.*
rŏt-a, ae, 1, *f., a wheel.*
Salvător, ŏris, 3, *m., The Saviour.*
sanguis, ĭnis, 3, *m., blood.*
săpienti-a, ae, 1, *f., wisdom.*
sŏl, sŏl-is, 3, *m., the sun.*
terra, ae, 1, *f., the earth.*
tĭmor, ŏris, 3, *m., fear.*
urbs, urb-is, 3, *f., a city.*
virtus, ûtis, 3, *f., virtue.*

1. Lux mundi. 2. Timor Domini. 3. Initium sapientiae. 4. REX JUDAEORUM. 5. Filius Dei. 6. Filius hominis. 7. Nomen Domini. 8. Angeli Dei. 9. Sanguis Jesu[1] Christi. 10. Panis vitae. 11. Salvator mundi. 12. Ovium greges. 13. Oculi Domini. 14. Fratres hominis hujus. 15. Verbum Dei.

16. Agnus Dei. 17. Filius amici mei. 18. Parentes hujus puellae. 19. Equus filii tui. 20. Manûs filiorum meorum. 21. Libri puerorum horum. 22. Horti amicorum nostrorum. 23. Pars vitae.[2] 24. Oculi magistrorum. 25. Lux solis. 26. Calor solis. 27. Libri magistrorum. 28. Vox filiae. 29. Creator mundi. 30. Domus patris.

31. Nomen regis. 32. Rotae curruum. 33. Urbis porta. 34. Praemium virtutis. 35. Templum Domini. 36. Aqua vitae. 37. Magnus numerus militum. 38. Quattuor millia hominum.[3] 39. Hujus hominis filia. 40. Corona vitae. 41. Domini est terra.[4] 42. Hoc est donum Dei.[5] 43. Tertia pars solis, et tertia pars lunae.[6] 44. Quorum primus ego sum.[7] 45. O mucro Domini.[8]

[1] See § 14 note. [2] § 97. [3] § 25, note 3, and § 97. [4] See § 96, a. [5] See § 96, b. [6] See § 97, a. [7] See § 97, b. [8] See § 115, a.

EXERCISE VII.

The Verb Sum. §§ 33—41.

Agrĭcŏl-a, ae, 1, m., a husbandman.
cert-us, a, um, certain.
dulc-is, e, sweet.
et, conj., and.
incert-us, a, um. uncertain.
mansi-o, ōnis, 3 f., a mansion.

mortal-is, e, mortal.
sāl, sālis, m. and n., salt.
somn-us, i, 2, m., sleep.
vēritas, ātis, 3, f., truth.
ver-us, a, um, true.
vīt-is, is, 3, f., a vine.

1. Homo sum.[1]   2. Rex est bonus.   3. Via longa est.
4. Vita brevis est.   5. Ego sum pastor bonus.[2]   6. Bona
est lex.[3]   7. Mors est certa.   8. Tempus incertum est.   9.
Non ego sum pastor.   10. Spiritus est Deus.[4]   11. Vos
amici mei estis.[5]   12. Ego sum panis vitae [6]

13. Dulcis est somnus.   14. Hic liber est meus.   15.
Deus est creator mundi.   16. Tu es spes mea.[7]   17. Vos
estis lux mundi.   18. Vos estis sal terrae.[8]   19. Ego sum
via, et veritas, et vita.   20. Tu es Filius meus dilectus.[9]
21. Tempus breve est.   22. Ego sum vitis vera, et Pater
meus agricola est.   23. Deus meus es tu.   24. HIC EST
JESUS REX JUDAEORUM.   25. In domo Patris mei man-
siones multae sunt.[10]

[1] Rule § 86, note.   [2] See § 90, a.   [3] See § 86, b.   [4] See § 86, c.   [5] See
§ 90 e.   [6] See § 95, a.   [7] See § 90 b.   [8] See § 85, b.   [9] See § 90, d   [10] See
§ 119.

EXERCISE VIII.

The Verb Sum—continued.

Antiŏchĭ-a, ae, Antioch.
beāt-us, a, um, happy.
cārĭtas, ātis, 3, f., love.
Ecclesi-a, ae, 1, f., the Church.
explōrātor, ōris, 3, m., a spy.
hŏnor, ōris, 3, m., honour.

impi-us, a, um, wicked.
palm-es, ĭtis, 3, m., a branch.
pax, pāc-is, 3, f., peace.
splendĭd-us, a, um, splendid.
ubĭ? adv., where?
vīv-us, a, um, living.

1. Tu es Christus Filius Dei vivi.[1]   2. Homo es.   3. Ego
sum vitis, vos palmites.   4. Quis est iste Filius hominis?
5. Initium sapientiae (est) timor Domini.   6. Ubi est ille?
7. Omnes filii unius viri sumus.[2]   8. Exploratores estis.
9. Non est pax impiis.   10. Dei estis.   11. Deus caritas
est.   12. Non est haec via.   13. Tuus amicus ero.   14.
Esto diligens.   15. Este boni pueri.

16. Tempus erat. 17. Milites fortes sunt. 18. Milites fortes sunt, boni sunto. 19. Cujus filius es tu? 20. Omnes boni beati sunt.[3] 21. Homines mortales sunt. 22. Liber est utilis. 23. Opus est utile. 24. Templum est splendidum. 25. Via est facilis. 26. Honor est praemium virtutis. 27. Haec nostra vita est brevissima. 28. Ubi es?[4] 29. Ubi est frater tuus? 30. In Ecclesiâ quae erat Antiochiae.[5] 31. Cum Apollos esset Corinthi.[6]

[1] Rule § 87. [2] See § 94, a. [3] See § 128. [4] See § 129, b. [5] See § 100, a. [6] See § 100, b, cum when, governs the Subjunctive Mood. *Corinth-us*, i., 2 m. Corinth.

EXERCISE IX.

The First Conjugation, Active Voice. §§ 42, 43.

Adŏr-o, āvi, ātum, āre, 1, *to worship.*
aedĭfĭc-o, avi, atum, are, 1, *to build.*
ăger, agr-i, 2, *m., a field.*
ambŭl-o, avi, atum, are 1, *to walk.*
ăm-o, avi, atum, are, 1, *to love.*
ar-o, avi, atum, are, 1, *to plough.*
av-is, av-is, 3, *f., a bird.*
cant-o, avi, atum, are, 1. *to sing.*
clam-o, āvi, ātum, āre, 1, *to cry out.*
di-es, ei, 5, *a day.* See § 15.
d-o, dĕdi, dātum, dăre, 1, *to give.*
fl-o, flavi, flatum, flare, 1, *to blow.*
in, prep. with abl., *in.*
intro, avi, atum, are, *to enter.*
jur-o, avi, atum, are, *to swear.*
laud-o, āvi, ātum, āre, 1, *to praise.*

mens-is, is, 3, *m., a month.*
naut-a, ae, 1, *m., a sailor.*
navig-o, avi, atum, are, 1, *to sail.*
or-o, avi, atum, are, 1, *to pray.*
pugn-o, avi, atum, are, *to fight.*
quis, quae, quid (quod), *who, which, what.*
secund-us, a, um, *second.*
sed, conj., *but.*
semper, adv., *always.*
septim-us, a, um, *seventh.*
vent-us, i, 2, *m., the wind.*
vigesim-us, a, um, *twentieth.*
virg-o, inis, 3, *f., a virgin.*
voc-o, avi, atum, are, 1, *to call.*
vol-o, avi, atum, are, 1, *to fly.*

1. Pater amat Filium.[1] 2. Agricola arat. 3. Avis volat. 4. Amamus Deum. 5. Vocat te. 6. Aedificat domum. 7. Puer jurat. 8. Magister bonos pueros laudat. 9. Boni pueri semper orant. 10. Laudamus te. 11. Adoramus te. 12. Adoramus Deum.

13. Magistri eum amant. 14. Omnes clamant. 15. Amicos meos amo. 16. Amicos nostros amamus. 17. Te amo. 18. Puellae cantabant. 19. Virgines cantant. 20. Mater filium laudabat. 21. Deus omnes amat; sed non omnes Deum amant. 22. Mater laudabat filias. 23. Deus dat vitam. 24. Pater librum dat puero.

F

25. Milites urbem intrant. 26. Domos in urbe aedificabant.[2] 27. Nauta navigat. 28. Ventus flabat. 29. Avis in arbore cantabat. 30. Quis nos vocat? 31. Milites pugnabant. 32. Libros dant magistro.[3] 33. Agricolae agros arant. 34. Jesus ambulabat in templo. 35. Agricolae ambulabant in hortis. 36. Mense secundo, septimo et vigesimo die mensis.[4]

[1] Rule, § 107.   [2] Rule § 119.   [3] Rule § 101.   [4] See § 120.

EXERCISE X.

The First Conjugation, Active Voice—continued.

Arēn-a, ae, 1, *f.*, *sand.*
coel-um, i, 2, *n.*, *heaven.*
cŏram, prep. with abl , *before.*
cre-o, avi, atum, are, 1, *to create.*
err-o, avi, atum, are, 1, *to err.*
in, prep. with acc., *against.*
ipse, ipsa, ipsum, *himself, herself, itself.*

judic-o. avi, atum are, 1, *to judge.*
pecc-o, avi, atum, are, 1, *to sin.*
per, prep. with acc., *through.*
praeceptor, ŏris, 3, *m.*, *a teacher.*
quia, conj., *because.*
recte, adv., *rightly.*
sper-o, avi, atum, are, 1, *to hope.*
stult-us, a, um, *foolish.*

super, prep. with acc., *upon.*

1. Aedificavi domum. 2. Amabo te. 3. Creavit Deus hominem. 4. Deus nos creavit. 5. Deus coelum et terram creavit. 6. Puer juraverat. 7. Agricolae arabunt agros. 8. Judicabit Dominus populum suum. 9. Ipse Pater amat vos, quia vos me amastis.[1] 10. Omnes peccavērunt. 11. Erravimus. 12. Magister pueros vocaverit.

13. Puer peccaverat. 14. Virgines cantabunt. 15. Semper amavi praeceptores meos. 16. Dominus juravit. 17. Pater, peccavi in coelum et coram te.[2] 18. Arabo. 19. Recte judicasti.[1] 20. Flavēre venti.[3] 21. Stultus aedificavit domum suam super arenam. 22. Speravi. 23. Quis malos pueros amabit? 24. Per urbem ambulavit. 25. Aquam pedibus meis non dedisti.[4]

[1] See § 60.   [2] § 75.   [3] § 61.   [4] § 101.

EXERCISE XI.

The First Conjugation, Active Voice—continued.

Ergo, conj., *therefore.*
exspecto, avi, atum, are, 1, *to wait.*
hŏnŏr-o, avi, atum, are, 1, *to honour.*
intermissīo, ōnis, 3, *f., ceasing.*
pro, prep. with abl., *for.*

sanct-us, a, um, *holy;* sanct-i, orum, pl., *the saints.*
sine, prep. with abl., *without.*
ut, conj., *that.*
vigil-o, avi, atum, are, 1, *to watch.*

1. Oremus. 2. Amemus Deum. 3. Aedificemus domum. 4. Amato patrem et matrem. 5. Araturus est. 6. Vigilate ergo. 7. Vigilate et orate. 8. Honora patrem tuum et matrem tuam. 9. Sine intermissione orate. 10. Fratres, orate pro nobis. 11. Et adorent eum angeli Dei omnes.

12. Milites pugnavissent. 13. Puer arato. 14. Laudate nomen Domini. 15. Agros araturus. 16. Arans. 17. Vigilans. 18. Lauda Dominum. 19. Agricolae aranto. 20. Ut ambularent per urbem. 21. Ama parentes. 22. Orantes et cantantes. 23. Orare et cantare. 24. Vigilare et orare.

25. Laudans Deum.[1] 26. Vocate agricolas. 27. O pueri! amate preceptores. 28. O mi amici, amatote Deum. 29. Amare Deum. 30. Agrum arare. 31. Laudare Dominum. 32. Aravisse agros. 33. Orare pro parentibus. 34. Orare pro omnibus. 35. Paulus autem cum Athenis eos exspectaret.[2] 36. Omnibus sanctis qui sunt Philippis.[3]

[1] Rule § 140. [2] See § 100 *c, Athēn-ae, arum,* 1, pl., Athens. [3] See § 100 *d.*

EXERCISE XII.

The Second Conjugation, Active Voice. §§ 44, 45.

Aut, conj., *or.*
autem, conj., *but, and.*
bĕāt-us, a, um, *blessed.*
caec-us, a, um, *blind.*
dŏc-ĕo, docui, doctum, docēre, 2, *to teach.*
ĕnim, conj., *for.*
fŏve-a, ae, 1, *f., a hole.*
hăb-eo, ui, itum, ēre, 2, *to have.*
luc-eo, luxi, lucēre, 2, *to shine.*
mors, mort-is, 3, *f., death.*
nīd-us, i, 2, *m., a nest.*
non, adv., *not.*
non solum, *not only.*

pān-is, pān-is, 3, *m., a loaf.*
pauc-us, a, um, *few.*
pauper, pauper-is, *poor.*
piscīcŭl-us, i, 2, *m., a little fish.*
qui, quae, quod, *who, which.*
quot? *how many?*
sed etiam, *but also.*
septem, num. adj., *seven.*
tim-eo, ui, ēre, 2, *to fear.*
vĕlut, adv., *as.*
video, vidi, visum, vidēre, 2, *to see.*
vŏlūcris, is, 3, *f., a bird.*
vulpes, is, 3, *f., a fox.*

1. Magister docet. 2. Magistri docent. 3. Et lux lucet. 4. Magister pueros docebant. 5. Deus nos videt. 6. Sol lucet. 7. Tune[1] times mortem? 8. Vos videtis. 9. Librum habeo. 10. Beati omnes qui timent Dominum. 11. Qui Deum timet, homines non timet. 12. Qui habet Filium habet vitam : qui non habet Filium, non habet vitam. 13. Pauperes enim semper habetis vobiscum ; me autem non semper habetis.

14. Quot habetis panes? Septem et paucos pisciculos. 15. Vulpes foveas habent, et volucres coeli nidos (habent). 16. Pater filiam suam docebat. 17. Jesus docet. 18. Mortem semper timebat. 19. Aves nidos habent. 20. Caeci non vident. 21. Agricolae agros habent. 22. Reges hortos habent. 23. Non solum domum sed etiam agros habemus. 24. Video homines velut arbōres ambulantes. 25. Habetisne[1] patrem aut fratrem? 26. Alias oves habeo.

[1] The particle *ne* joined on to the first word of a sentence is not to be translated, but is used to show that a question is asked ; as, *Tune times mortem?* Dost thou fear death?

EXERCISE XIII.

The Second Conjugation, Active Voice—continued.

Eg-eo, ui, 2, *to be in need of anything.*
fic-us, us, 4, *f., a fig-tree.*
hydri-a, ae, 1, *f., a water-pot.*
impl-eo, ēvi, ētum, ēre, 2, *to fill.*
leo, ōnis, 3, *m., a lion.*
lucern-a, ae, 1, *f., a candle.*
lumen, lumin-is, 8, *n., light.*

man-eo, man-si, mans-um, ēre, 2, *to remain.*
mon-eo, ui, ĭtum, ēre, 2, *to advise.*
nēmo, nemĭn-is, 3, *c., no one.*
neque, conj., *neither.*
noc-eo, ui, ĭtum, ēre, 2, *to hurt.*
sub, prep. with abl., *under.*

unquam, adv., *at any time.*

1. Pater docuit filium. 2. Preceptores pueros monuerunt. 3. Vidi te. 4. Et ego vidi. 5. Vidi te sub ficu. 6. Videbit eum omnis oculus. 7. Ego videbo filium meum. 8. Dominum vidimus. 9. Deum nemo vidit unquam. 10. Rex urbem videbit. 11. Solem vidisti. 12. Illi pueros monuēre (monuerunt),[1] ego preceptores monebo. 13. Mulier implevit hydrias aquā. 14. Magistrumne[2] ⸱⸱disti? 15. Leones non nocuerunt mihi.[3] 16. Et mansit

ibi duos dies.[4] 17. Non egebunt lumine lucernae, neque lumine solis.[5]

[1] See § 61. [2] See Exercise XII., note. [3] See § 102, d. [4] See § 110 [5] See § 123, b.

EXERCISE XIV.

The Second Conjugation, Active Voice—continued.

Ars, art-is, 3, f., art. | dĕb-eo, deb-ui, deb-ĭtum, deb-ēre, 2, I ought.
tăc-eo, ui, ĭtum, ēre, 2, to be silent.

1. Time Dominum. 2. Deum timete. 3. Doceamus hos pueros. 4. Mone puerum. 5. Quis has malas puellas docuisset? 6. Doce me. 7. Omnes homines mortales sunt; ergo omnes mortem timēre debent. 8. Ars docendi difficilis est. 9. Ars navigandi difficilis est. 10. Implete hydrias aquā. 11. Et impleverunt eas. 12. Time Dominum, fili mi, et regem.[1] 13. Doceamus hos pueros. 14. Docete puellas. 15. Pueri bonos libros habeant. 16. Tacete, O pueri. 17. Amare Deum debemus. 18. Magistri monēre pueros debent. 19. Timens, monens, docens. 20. Monuisse puellas.

[1] The Vocative Singular of meus is mi, and of filius, fili: see § 28, note

---

EXERCISE XV.

The Third Conjugation, Active Voice. §§ 46, 47.

Ad, prep. with acc., to.
bĭb-o, bĭb-i, bĭb-ĭtum, bĭb-ĕre, 3, to drink.
cresc-o, crēv-i, crēt-um, cresc-ĕre, 3, to grow.
curr-o, cŭcurr-i, curs-um, curr-ĕre, 3, to run.
dīc-o, dix-i, dict-um, dīc-ĕre, 3, to say.
dīlĭg-o, dīlex-i, dīlect-um, dīlig-ĕre, 3, to love.
disc-o, didic-i, ——, disc-ĕre, 3, to learn.
ecce, conj., behold.
ego, I. § 27.
flŭ-o, flux-i, flux-um, flu-ĕre, 3, to flow.
in, prep., with abl., upon; with acc., into.

lĕg-o, lĕg-i, lect-um, lĕg-ĕre, 3, to read.
lūd-o, lūs-i, lūs-um, lūd-ĕre, 3, to play.
mitt-o, mis-i, miss-um, mitt-ĕre, 3, to send.
nec-nec, neither-nor.
pasc-o, pāv-i, past-um, pasc-ĕre, 3, to feed.
per, prep. with acc., through.
rĕg-o, rex-i, rect-um, rĕg-ĕre, 3, to rule.
scrĭb-o, scrips-i, script-um, scrĭb-ĕre, 3, to write.
se, himself. § 27.
silv-a, ae, 1, f., a wood.
sŏror, sŏrōr-is, 3, f., a sister.
văd-o, văs-i, văs-um, văd-ĕre, 3, to go.

vinc-o, vic-i, vict-um, vinc-ĕre, 3, to conquer.

1. Puer lĕgit.   2. Puella scribit epistolam.   3. Soror ludit.   4. Ego curro.   5. Arbor crescit.   6. Agricola pascit oves et boves.   7. Vado ad Patrem.   8. Labor omnia vincit.   9. Puer currebat.   10. Quid dicis?   11. Magister dicit.   12. Equus currit.   13. Pueri discunt.   14. Milites in urbem currunt.[1]   15. Deus regit mundum.

16. Nec scribit, nec lĕgit.   17. Fratres tui pascunt oves.   18. Aqua fluit.   19. Fortis est qui se vincit.   20. Soror fratrem diligit.   21. Equi currunt per silvas et agros.   22. Arbŏres crescunt.   23. Ecce ego mitto angelum meum.   24. Dominus regit.   25. Vos bibitis vinum : nos aquam bibimus.   26. Pueri pascebant oves in montibus.   27. Magister puerum mittit.   28. Magistri vinum bibunt.   29. Puellae bibunt aquam.   30. Pastores in urbem vadunt.   31. Scribae dicunt.   32. Quem dicunt homines esse Filium hominis?[2]

[1] See § 112.   [2] See § 113, a.

EXERCISE XVI.

The Third Conjugation, Active Voice—continued.

Crĕd-o, crĕdĭ l-i, crĕdĭt-um, crĕ l-ĕre, 3, *to believe.*
discĭpŭl-us, i, 2, *m., a pupil.*
dŭc-o, dux-i, duct-um, dŭc-ĕre, 3, *to lead.*
ĕlĭg-o, ĕlĕg-i, ĕlect-um, ĕlĭg-ĕre, 3, *to choose.*
ex, prep. with abl , *(out) of.*
hŏdie, adv., *to-day.*
ĭ. terrŏg-o, avi, atum, are, 1, *to ask.*

mandŭc-o, avi, atum, are, 1, *to eat.*
nunc, adv., *now.*
Pilāt-us, i, 2, *m., Pilate.*
quŏ, adv., *whither.*
rĕsurg-o, rĕsurrex-i, rĕsurrect-um, rĕsurg-ĕr , 3, *to rise again.*
sed, conj., *but.*
sīcŭt, adv., *like.*
tang-o, tĕtĭg-i, tact-um, tang-ĕre, 3, *to touch.*

1. Lĕgi tuas epistolas.   2. Magistri dixerunt.   3. Puer longam epistolam scribet.   4. Has epistolas scripsi.   5. Et nunc vado ad eum qui misit me ; et nemo ex vobis interrogat me : Quo vadis?   6. Qui videt me, videt eum qui misit me.   7. Resurget frater tuus.[1]   8. Et duxerunt illum ad Pilatum.   9. Ego pascam oves meas.   10. Sicut pastor gregem suum pascet.   11. Non vos me elegistis ; sed ego elĕgi vos.[2]   12. Filium meum mittam.

13. Dominus misit me ad te. 14. Quid manducabimus, quid bibemus? 15. Quis me tetigit?[3] 16. Hanc epistolam meā manu scripsi. 17. Hunc librum lēgi. 18. Puer discet. 19. Discipulus epistolam suā manu scripserat. 20. Pueri dixerunt. 21. Hodie epistolam scripsi. 22. Epistolas lēgi quas scripsisti.[4] 23. Panem manducaverant. 24. Aquam biberant. 25. Vinum bibent. 26. Ego vēni ut vitam habeant.

[1] See § 134.　　[2] See § 88.　　[3] See § 132.　　[4] See § 91.

EXERCISE XVII.

The Third Conjugation, Active Voice—continued.

Ascend-o, ascend-i, ascens-um, as-cend-ēre, 3, to ascend.
bĕne, adv., well.
bĭs, adv, twice.
content-us, a, um, content.
crūcĭfīg-o crucifix-i, crucifix-um, cruciflg-ēre, 3, to crucify.
cŭp-io, ĭvi and ii, ĭtum, ĕre, 3, to desire. § 69.
dă, give, imp. 2 s. of do.
dic, tell, say, imp. 2 s. of dico. § 69 (Obs.).
dīlĭgens, ntis, loving, pres. part. of dīlĭgo.
discĭpŭl-us, i, 2, m., a disciple.
disced-o, discess-i, discess-um, dis-cod-ēre, 3, to depart.
esse, to be, infin. pres. of sum.
frātərnĭtas, ātis, 3, f., brotherhood.

hŏnōrĭfĭc-o, avi, atum, are, 1, to honour.
ignosc-o, nōv-i, nōt-um, nosc-ēre, 3, to pardon.
illĭc, adv., there.
inĭmīc-us, i, 2, m., an enemy.
ĭtĕrum, adv., again.
măgis, adv., more.
oscul-um, i, 2, n., a kiss.
parv-us, a, um, little.
Petr-us, i, 2, m., Peter.
quam, adv., than.
scriptūr-us, a, um, about to write, fut. part. of scribo.
surg-o, surrex-i, surrect-um, surg-ēre, 3, to rise.
trād-o, dĭdi, dĭtum, ĕre, 3, to betray.
vīv-o, vix-i, vict-um, vīv-ēre, 3, to live.

1. Lege bonos libros. 2. Vade in pace. 3. Pasce oves meas. 4. Pasce agnos meos. 5. Vade ad fratres meos, et dic[1] eis: "Ascendo ad Patrem meum et Patrem vestrum, Deum meum et Deum vestrum." 6. Da mihi librum. 7. Da mihi bibĕre. 8. Diligite inimicos vestros. 9. Omnes honorate: fraternitatem diligite: Deum timete: regem honorificate. 10. Illi iterum clamaverunt: "Crucifige eum." Et crucifixerunt eum. 11. Vade, filius tuus vivit. 12. Manducemus et bibamus.

13. Et Jesus interrogabat discipulos suos, dicens: "Quem dicunt homines esse Filium hominis?"   14. Dicit illis Jesus: "Vos autem quem me esse dicitis?"   Respondens Simon Petrus dixit: "Tu es Christus, Filius Dei vivi." 15. Ego diligentes² me diligo.   16. Quod vides, scrībe in libro.   17. Scribe ergo quae vidisti.   18. Ut epistolas scribamus.   19. Libros bonos legamus.   20. Epistolam scripturus.   21. Omnes *(we all)* cupimus te vidēre.   22. Surge.   23. Bene vivĕre, bis vivĕre est; bene vivite.   24. Bonos libros legĕre amo.

25. Non facile³ est longas epistolas scribĕre.   26. Facile est scribĕre, non facile est bene scribĕre.   27. Docendo discimus.   28. Puer ludendo non discit.   29. Te scribentem vidi.   30. Disce aut discede.   31. Disce scribĕre.   32. Disce parvo esse contentus.⁴   33. Pueri scribunto.   34. Discite legĕre bonos libros.   35. Docet pueros, ut legĕre discant.   36. Lēgit, ut discat.

37. Legat, ut discat.   38. Scribant pueri.   39. Discĕre est utile.   40. Discat puer legĕre.   41. Equus currito. 42. Ars scribendi utilis est.   43. Venite et videte.   44. Pueri ludant.   45. Petrus et Joannes ascendebant in templum.   46. Quia ego vivo; et vos vivetis.⁵   47. Da mihi hanc aquam.⁶   48. Ignoscat mihi Dominus servo tuo.⁷ 49. Ecce ascendimus Jerosolymam.⁸   50. Juda, osculo Filium hominis tradis?⁹   51. Si ascendero coelum, tu illic es.¹⁰   52. Si quo minus, dixissem vobis.¹¹

¹ See § 69, obs. ² *Ego diligo*, I love; *diligentes me*, them that love me: see § 141. ³ *Non facile est*, it is not easy, *i.e.*, it is not an easy (thing); see § 128. ⁴ See § 124. ⁵ See § 93. ⁶ See § 102, *a.* ⁷ See § 102, *c.* ⁸ See § 111, *a.* ⁹ See § 117, *b.* ¹⁰ See § 135, *b.* ¹¹ See § 136, *a*; *Si quo minus,* if it were not so.

EXERCISE XVIII.

The Fourth Conjugation, Active Voice. §§ *48 and 49.*

Adŏlescens, ntis, 3. *m.*, *a young man.*
an.n-us, i, 2, *m.*, *a year.*
ă,·ĕr-Io, ivi, Itum, Ire, 4, *to open.*
aud-io, ivi, Itum, Ire, 4, *to hear.*
cum, prep. with abl., *with.*
dorm-io, ivi, Itum, Ire, 4, *to sleep.*
ŏsŭr-io, ivi, Itum, Ire, 4, *to hunger.*
hŏr-a, ae, 1, *f.*, *an hour.*
nŭb-es, is, 3, *f.*, *a cloud.* § 13.
obdorm-io, ivi, Itum, Ire, 4, *to fall asleep.*

pūn-io, ivi, Itum, Ire, 4, *to punish.*
sc-io, ivi, Itum, Ire, 4, *to know.*
sent-io, sens-i, sens-um, sent-Ire, 4, *to feel.*
sepel-io, ivi, Itum, Ire, 4, *to bury.*
sĭt-io, ivi, Itum, Ire, 4, *to thirst.*
somniător, ŏris, 3, *m.*, *a dreamer.*
surd-us, a, um, *deaf.*
unquam, adv., *ever.*
vĕn-io, vĕn-i, vent-um, vĕn-Ire, 4, *to come.*

1. Nox vĕnit. 2. Vĕnit hora. 3. Amicus noster dormit. 4. Puella dormit. 5. Tu dormis. 6. Ecce rex tuus vĕnit. 7. Qui *(those who)* dormiunt, nocte dormiunt. 8. Agricola dormiebat. 9. Anno Domini (A.D.). 10. Anno Mundi (A.M.). 11. Anno quarto. 12. Quis vĕnit? 13. Hominis vocem audio.

14. Veni, vidi, vici. 15. Audisne?[1] 16. Puer audit vocem. 17. Magistri audient vocem. 18. Mors vĕnit. 19. Ecce somniator vĕnit. 20. Veniėsne mecum? 21. Et alius angelus vĕnit. 22. Oves meae vocem meam audiunt. 23. Audivi vocem. 24. Veneruntque ad eum fratres sui.

25. Pater tuus et fratres tui venerunt ad te. 26. Magister librum aperiet. 27. Ego te non punivi. 28. Venerunt ad me duo adolescentes. 29. Christus Jesus vĕnit in hunc mundum. 30. Dixit autem eis Jesus: "Ego sum panis vitae; qui[2] vĕnit ad me, non esuriet; et qui credit in me, non sitiet unquam." 31. Scio eum esse mendacem hominem. 32. Pater filium sepeliverat. 33. Surdi non audiunt. 34. Calorem solis hodie sentimus. 35. Agricola filium hodie sepeliit. 36. Ecce vĕnit cum nubibus; et videbit eum omnis oculus. 37. Mense primo, primā die mensis.[3] 38. Navigantibus illis, obdormivit.[4] 39. Omnes scient me.[5]

---

[1] See Exercise XII., note. [2] *Qui*, he that. [3] See § 120. [4] See § 126, b. [5] See § 128, a.

EXERCISE XIX.

The Fourth Conjugation, Active Voice—continued.

Alter, era, erum, *the other.*
auris, is, 3, *f.*, *an ear.*
cãr-us, a, um, *dear.*
dign-us, a, um, *worthy.*
diligenter, adv., *carefully.*
disciplin-a, ae, 1, *f.*, *instruction.*
ĕrŭd-io, ivi, itum, ire, 4, *to instruct.*
esuriens, ntis, *hungry* (pres. part. of esurio).
gladi-us, i, 2, *m.*, *a sword.*
hērēdĭtas, ātis, 3, *f.*, *an inheritance.*
hēres, ēdis, 3, *m.*, *an heir.*
hūc, adv., *hither.*

invĕn-io, vēni, ventum, ire, 4, *to find.*
Jacob-us, i, 2, *m.*, *James.*
Joann-es, is, 3, *m.*, *John.*
Magi, *wise men.*
majestas, atis, 3, *f.*, *glory.*
occĭd-o, occĭd-i, occĭs-um, occĭd-ēre, 3, *to kill, slay.*
Oriens, ntis, *the East.*
ōs, ōr-is, 3, *n.*, *a mouth.*
sanct-us, a, um, *holy.*
serv-us, i, 2, *m.*, *a servant.*
ventūrus est, *is to come* (fut. part of venio).

1. Ego cupio ad te venire. 2. Quis est dignus aperire librum? 3. Vĕni huc. 4. Veniat ad me. 5. Vĕni in hortum meum. 6. Aperite portas. 7. Aperi os tuum. 8. Puni malos pueros. 9. Auditote meam vocem. 10. Me amatis: ad me venite. 11. Audi alteram partem. 12. Pueri diligenter erudiendi sunt. 13. Aperite urbis portas.

14. Et vĕnit ad discipulos et invĕnit eos dormientes. 15. Et vēnit iterum, et invĕnit eos dormientes. 16. Hic est Filius meus carissimus: audīte illum. 17. Dico huic: Vade, et vadit; et alii: Vĕni, et vĕnit. 18. Hic est heres; venite, occidamus eum, et habebimus hereditatem ejus. 19. Aperi oculos hujus pueri. 20. Aperi oculos istorum, ut videant. 21. Oculos habentes nonne videtis? et aures habentes nonne auditis? 22. Aperi oculos tuos. 23. Venite in urbem. 24. Sanctus, sanctus, sanctus, Dominus Deus omnipotens, qui erat, qui est, et qui venturus est. 25. Occĭdit autem Jacobum, fratrem Joannis gladio.[1] 26. Vĕni mecum domum.[2] 27. Audite, filii, disciplinam patris. 28. Ecce Magi ab Oriente venērunt. 29. Esurientes implevit bonis.[3] 30. Cum venerit Filius hominis in . majestate suā.[4]

See § 87, *a*, and § 117, *a*.   [2] See § 111, *b*.   [3] See § 123, *a*.   [4] See § 125.

EXERCISE XX.

The First Conjugation, Passive Voice. §§ 50, 51.

A, ab, abs, prep. with abl., *by*.
ărăt-us, *ploughed* (past part. of aro).
autem, conj., *for*.
cert-us, a, um, *certain*.
cito, adv., *quickly*.
culp-o, avi, atum, are, 1, *to blame*.
dătum, *given* (past part. of do).
dĕlect-o, avi, atum, are, 1, *to delight*.
exalt-o, avi, atum, are, 1, *to exalt*.
humilĭ-o, avi, atum, are, 1, *to humble*.
invĭtăt-us, a, um, *bidden* (past part. of invit-o, avi, atum, are, 1, *to invite, bid*).
jam non, *no more*.

melius, neut. comp. of bon-us, a, um. § 19.
mut-o, avi, atum, are, 1, *to change*.
nunquam, adv., *never*.
nupti-ae, arum, 1, *f.* plur., *wedding*.
ōrātio, ōnis, 3, *f.*, *prayer*.
quia, conj., *for*.
saepe, adv., *often*.
si, conj., *if*.
sperăt-us, a, um, *hoped for* (past part. of sper-o, avi, atum, are, 1, *to hope for*).
valde, adv., *very much*.
victōri-a, ae, 1, *f.*, *victory*.

1. Agri arantur. 2. Parentes a filiis amantur.[1] 3. Ego nunquam laudor : tu semper laudaris. 4. Pueri boni laudabantur. 5. Homines judicantur. 6. Puer judicetur. 7. Filius a patre amatur. 8. Mali culpantur : laudantur boni. 9. Melius est certa pax, quam sperata victoria. 10. Tempora mutantur, et nos mutamur in illis. 11. Si bonus es, laudaberis. 12. Domus magistri cito aedificabitur. 13. Domus mea domus orationis vocabitur.

14. Jam non sum dignus vocari filius tuus. 15. Nec vocemini magistri : quia Magister vester unus est, Christus. 16. Qui autem se exaltaverit, humiliabitur ; et qui se humiliaverit, exaltabitur. 17. Mater mea valde delectatur. 18. Hic ager bene aratus est. 19. Domus aedificata est. 20. Vinum pauperibus datum erat. 21. Laudatur ab his : culpatur ab illis. ·22. A patre meo laudatus sum. 23. Quis a te laudabitur ? 24. Nemo culpator. 25. Boni pueri laudantor. 26. Melius est laudari, quam culpari. 27. Et rex misit servos suos vocare invitatos ad nuptias. 28. Filius Altissimi vocabitur.[2]

[1] Rule, § 118.   [2] See § 94, c.

EXERCISE XXI.

The Second Conjugation, Passive Voice. §§ 52, 53.

Content-us, a, um, *content.*
dīligens, ntis, *diligent.*
lĕgio, ōnis, 3, *f.*, *a legion.*
merces, ēdis, 3, *f.*, *reward.*
must-um, i, 2, *n.*, *new wine.*

ŏpĕrārius, 2, *m.*, *a labourer.*
plēn-us, a, um, *full.*
stipendi-a, 2, *n.*, pl., *wages.*
terr-eo, ui, ĭtum, ēre, 2, *to frighten.*

1. Pueri a magistris docentur.   2. Pueri diligenter docentor.   3. A magistro doctus sum.   4. Mali timentur : amantur boni.   5. Boni non timebuntur.   6. Filiae a patre docebantur.   7. Discipuli a magistro docti essent.   8. Magistri ab omnibus discipulis timebantur.   9. Moniti sumus ut diligentiores essemus.   10. Pueri moniti essent. 11. Puellae territae erant.   12. Mulieres non terrebuntur. 13. Et interrogabat eum : " Quod tibi nomen est ?" Et dicit ei : " Legio mihi nomen est quia multi sumus."   14. Musto pleni sunt isti.[1]   15. Dignus est operarius mercede suā.[2]   16. Contenti estote stipendiis vestris.[3]

[1] See § 123, c.   [2] See § 124, a.   [3] See § 124 b.

EXERCISE XXII.

The Third Conjugation, Passive Voice. §§ 54, 55.

Absorpt-us, a, um, *swallowed up* (past part. of absorb-eo, absorb-ui, and absorps-i, ptum, bĕre, 2, *to swallow up*).
ag-o, ēgi, actum, agĕre, 3, *to do, lead, drive.*
benedict-us, a, um, *blessed.*
desert-us, i, 2, *m.*, *a desert.*
duct-us, a, um, *led* (past part. of duco).

hostis, is, 3, *m.*, *an enemy.*
hostes, pl., *the enemy.*
lătro, ōnis, 3, *m.*, *a thief.*
liter-a, ae, 1, *f.*, *a letter.*
prophet-a, ae, 1, *m.*, *a prophet.*
script-us, a, um, *written* (past part. of scribo).
vict-us, a, um, *conquered* (past part. of vinc-o).

1. Ducuntur pueri.   2. Epistola mittetur.   3. Libri leguntur.   4. Libri legebantur.   5. Benedictus qui vĕnit in nomine Domini !   6. Dicunt omnes : Crucifigatur !   7. Absorpta est mors in victoria.   8. Crucifixi sunt, cum eo duo latrōnes.   9. Litera scripta manet.   10. Libri lecti erant.   11. Ars docendi discitur.   12. Mundus regitur a Deo.

13. Puella a matre docebatur. 14. Jesus crucifixus est.
15. Epistolae scriptae sunt. 16. Omnia labore vincuntur.
17. Frater a sororibus diligitur. 18. A rege missus sum.
19. Ductus est ad Pilatum. 20. Hostis vincitur. 21.
Milites! victi estis. 22. Et agebatur a Spiritu in desertum.[1]
23. Et mansit ibi duos dies.[2] 24. Non est servus major
domino suo.[3] 25. Neque enim melior sum quam patres
mei.[4] 26. Credens omnibus quae in lege et prophetis
scripta sunt.[5]

[1] See § 118. [2] See § 110. [3] See § 125 a. [4] See § 125, b. [5] See § 140 b.

EXERCISE XXIII.

The Fourth Conjugation, Passive Voice. §§ 56, 57.

An, *or.*
fīn-io, īvi, ītum, īre, 4, *to finish.*
impröb-us, a, um, *wicked.*
plac-eo, uī, ītum, ēre, 2, *to please.*
quaer-o, quaesīv-ī, quaesīt-um,
quaer-ēre, 8, *to seek.*

rĕpĕr-io, rĕpĕr-ī, rĕpert-um, rĕpĕr-
īre, 4, *to find.*
suadeo, sī, sum, ēre, 1, *to persuade.*
vest-io, īvi, ītum, īre, 4, *to clothe.*

1. Labor finitur. 2. Pueri erudiuntur. 3. Vox auditur.
4. Corpora sepeliuntur. 5. Labores finiti essent. 6.
Puellae a matre vestiebantur. 7. Hi duo pueri diligenter
a magistro eruditi sunt. 8. Puniuntor mali pueri. 9. Pueri
a magistris erudiuntur. 10. Corpora sepeliuntor. 11.
Mali pueri a magistro punientur. 12. Improbi homines a
Deo punientur. 13. Corpora sepelientur. 14. Haec nostra
vita reperietur brevissima. 15. Et aperti sunt oculi
amborum.[1] 16. Modo enim hominibus suadeo, an Deo?[2]
17. An quaero hominibus placēre?[3]

[1] See §§ 25, 95, b. [2] See § 102, g. [3] See § 102, e.

EXERCISE XXIV.

Verbs in IO of the Third Conjugation. § 69.

Accĭpio, cēpi, ceptum, cĭpĕre, 3, *to take, receive.*
bĕnĕdictio, ōnis, 3, *f., blessing.*
dăre, *to give* (pres. inf. of do).
dīvĭnĭtas, ātis, 3, *f., riches.*
făcio, fēci, factum, făcĕre, 3, *to do, make.*
fac, *do (thou),* imper., 2, sing. § 69, Obs.
flamm-a, ae, 1, *f., flame.*
fŏdio, fōdi, fossum, fŏdĕre, 3, *to dig.*
fortĭtūdo, dĭnis, 3, *f., strength.*
fŭgio, fŭgi, fŭgitum, fŭgĕre, 3, *to flee.*
glŏri-a, ae, 1, *f., glory.*

ignis, is, 3, *m., fire.*
mendĭc-o, avi, atum, are, 1, *to beg.*
minister, tri, 2, *m., a minister.*
occĭs-us, a, um, *slain* (past part. of occĭdo).
piscis, is, 3, *m., a fish.*
propter, prep. with acc., *for, on account of.*
sapienti-a, ae, 1, *f., wisdom.*
secundum, prep. with acc., *according to.*
simĭlĭter, adv., *likewise.*
super, prep. with acc., *upon.*
virtus, ūtis, 3, *f., power.*
vŏluntas, ātis, 3, *f., pleasure.*

1. Quis mundum fecit? 2. Bene omnia fēcit.[1] 3. Quid faciam (*fut.*)? 4. Avis nidum facit. 5. Quid fecisti? 6. Aves nidos in arboribus faciunt. 7. Hostes fugiunt. 8. Agricolae fodiunt. 9. Melius est fodĕre quam mendicare. 10. Epistolam tuam accēpi. 11. Multas a te accēpi epistolas, omnes diligenter scriptas. 12. Accēperam tuas epistolas.

13. Dico huic : Vade, et vadit ; et alii : Vĕni, et vĕnit ; et servo meo : Fac[2] hoc, et facit. 14. Dominus fecit mundum et omnia quae in eo sunt. 15. Beatius est dare quam accipĕre. 16. Ego feci terram, et hominem super eam creavi ego. 17. Vade, et tu fac similiter. 18. Hoc fac, et vives. 19. Qui facit angelos suos spiritūs, et ministros suos flammam ignis. 20. Dignus est Agnus, qui occisus est, accipĕre virtutem, et divinitatem, et sapientiam, et fortitudinem, et honorem, et gloriam, et benedictionem. 21. Dignus es, Domine Deus noster, accipĕre gloriam, et honorem, et virtutem, quia tu creasti omnia, et propter voluntatem tuam erant, et creata sunt. 22. Dixit ergo eis Pilatus : "Accipite eum, et secundum legem vestram[3] judicate eum." 23. Sunt alia multa, quae fēcit Jesus.[4] 24. Acceptis autem quinque panibus, et duobus piscibus.[5]

---

[1] See § 128, *b*. [2] *Fac hoc,* do this (thing). see § 69, obs. [3] *Secundum legem vestram,* according to your law. (See list of Prepositions, § 75.) [4] See § 91, *b*. [5] See § 126, *a*.

EXERCISE XXV.

Irregular Verbs. §§ 78 and 41, obs.

Ad-sum, *I am here.*
aetas, ātis, 3, *f.*, *age.*
aeternitas, ātis, 3, *f.*, *eternity.*
annŭlus, i, 2, *m.*, *a ring.*
claud-o, claus-i, claus-um, claud-ĕre, 3, *to shut.*
condemn-o, avi, atum, are, 1, *to condemn.*
confĕro, contŭli, collatum, conferre, *to compare;* confer, *compare (thou);* imper, 2, sing.
cor, cord-is, 3, *n.*, *the heart.*
crux, cruc-is, 3, *f.*, *a cross.*
desum, *I am wanting.*
form-o, avi, atum, are, 1, *to form.*
fruct-us, ûs, 4, *m.*, *fruit.*
fert fructum, *bringeth forth fruit.*
hinc, adv., *hence.*
intellig-o, intellex-i, intellect-um, intelligĕre, 3, *to understand.*
lābŏr-o, avi, atum, are, 1, *to labour.*
lapid-o, avi, atum, are, 1, *to stone.*
lăp-is, idis, 3, *m.*, *a stone.*
mund-us, a, um, *clean.*
neque, conj., *neither.*
nesc-io, ivi, itum, ire, *to know not.*
nihil, *nothing.*
nolo, *I am unwilling;* noli, imper., 2, sing., *be unwilling to,* i.e., *do not (thou);* plur., nolite, *do not (ye).*

ŏnĕrat-us, a, um, *heavy-laden.*
peccat-um, i, 2, *n.*, *sin.*
pōno, pŏsui, pŏsit-um, ponĕre, 3, *to lay.*
praeter-eo, ivi and ii, itum, ire, *to pass away.*
prohib-eo, ui, itum, ĕre 2, *to forbid.*
que, *and,* joined on to the end of the word.
re-ficio, fēci, fectum, ficĕre, 3, *to refresh.*
sine, prep., with abl., *without.*
surg-o, surrex-i, surrect-um, surgĕre, 3, *to rise.*
sĭn-o, sīvi, sĭtum, sĭnĕre, 3, *to let suffer.*
sinite (eum) abire, *allow him to go,* i.e., *let him go.*
solvo, solvi, sŏlūtum, solvĕre, 3, *to loose.*
sustoll-o, tuli, tol'ĕre, *to take up or away.*
toll-o, sustuli, sublatum, tollĕre, *to take up.*
trans-eo, ivi and ii, itum, ire, *to pass away.*
tulĕrunt, *they have taken away,* 3 pers. plur. perf. of sustollo.
verb-um, i, 2 *n.*, *a word.*

1. Scribĕre non possum. 2. Agricolae possunt agros arare. 3. Intelligĕre non potest. 4. Potestne[1] arăre? 5. Pueri voluerunt dormire. 6. Magister vult amari. 7. Vivĕre nolo. 8. Eamus ad urbem. 9. Surgite, eamus hinc. 10. Potestne[1] docēre? 11. Fodĕre non possumus. 12. Parva puella claudĕre portam non potest.

13. Volui dormire. 14. Magister semper adest. 15. Homines fiunt sapientes. 16. Vēnit ut portas claudat. 17. Vēnit ut portas clauderet. 18. Vēnit ut portas claudat. 19. Veniat ut portas claudat. 20. Venerat ut portas clauderet. 21. Ecce Agnus Dei, qui tollit peccatum mundi. 22. Eamus in urbem iterum. 23. Tollite lapidem. 24. Tulerunt lapidem. 25. Tulitque annulum de manu suā.

26. Noli me tangĕre.   27. Nolite peccare in puerum.[2]
28. Pax vobiscum, nolite timēre.   29. Nolite prohibēre
eum.   30. Caelum et terra transibunt, verba autem mea
non praeteribunt.   31. Nolite diligĕre mundum, neque
ea quae in mundo sunt.   32. Si quis diligit mundum, non
est caritas Patris in eo.   33. Sine me nihil potestis facĕre.
34. Ego sum vitis, vos palmites : qui manet in me, et ego
in eo, hic (*the same*) fert fructum multum.   35. Nolite
judicare.   36. Nolite judicare, et non judicabimini : nolite
condemnare, et non condemnabimini.

37. Venite ad me omnes qui[3] laboratis et onerati estis,
et ego reficiam vos.   38. Unum tibi deest.[4]   39. Tulerunt
Dominum meum, et nescio ubi posuerunt eum.   40.
Domine, si tu sustulisti eum, dicito mihi ubi posuisti eum;
et ego eum tollam.   41. Quis potest dicĕre : "Mundum
est cor meum?"   42. Noli timēre.   43. Nolite timēre.
44. Dixitque Dominus : "Fiat lux."[5]   Et facta est lux.
45. I! puer.   46. Vos ite domum : ego manebo.   47.
Surgam, et ibo ad patrem meum, et dicam ei : "Pater
peccavi in coelum et coram te ; jam non sum dignus
vocari filius tuus."   Et surgens,[6] vēnit ad patrem suum.
48. In domum Domini ibimus.

49. Noli aquam bibĕre.   50. Ut puer fiat bonus.   51.
Surdi non possunt audire : caeci non possunt vidēre.   52.
Confer nostram longissimam aetatem cum aeternitate, et
invenietur brevissima.   53. Ite et videte.   54. Et rex
misit servos suos vocare invitatos ad nuptias, et nolebant
venire.   55. Factus es populus Domini Dei tui.[7]   56. Et
nihil mihi deerit.[4]   57. Quid enim proderit homini ?[a]   58.
In quo posuit hominem quem formaverat.[8]   59. Sustul-
erunt lapides Judaei, ut lapidārent eum.[9]   60. Solvite
eum, et sinite abire.[10]

---

[1] *Pote-ne*, is he able? *i.e.*, can he?   [2] *In puerum*, against the lad, see §
75.   [3] *Qui*, ye that.   [4] See § 103.   [5] *Fiat lux*, let there be light.   [6] See §
141.   [7] See § 94, *b*.   [8] See § 133.   [9] See § 136, *b*.   [10] See § 139.

EXERCISE XXVI.

Deponent Verbs. § 70.

Arc-a, 1, *f.*, *the ark.*
cǎnis, is, 3, c., *a dog.*
cognosc-o, cognŏv-i, cognĭt-um, cognosc-ĕre, 3, *to know.*
cras, adv., *to-morrow.*
cum, *when.*
cunct-us, a, um, *all.*
de, prep with abl., *from.*
dens, dent-is, 3, *m.*, *a tooth.*
dicens, ntis, *saying* (pres. part. of dico).
dīmitt-o, mīsi, missum, mittĕre, 3, *to leave.*
et-et, *both-and.*

ex-eo, īvi, and ĭi, ĭtum, īre, *to come out.*
fru-or, fruĭt-us, fruct-us sum, fru-i, 3, dep., *to enjoy.*
hĕri, adv., *yesterday.*
hīc, adv., *here.*
modicus, a, um, *a little.*
nĭsi, *save, except.*
occĭdit sol, *the sun sets.*
pars, part-is, 3, *f.*, *a part, portion.*
sacerdoti-um, i, 2, *n.*, *the priest's office.*
turb-a, ae, 1, *f.*, *a multitude.*
unde, adv., *whence.*
vivens, entis, part., *living.*

1. Misereor amici mei.[1] 2. Miserēre nostri.[2] 3. Venerare Deum (Imper.). 4. Misereor turbae. 5. Homines hortati sunt. 6. Rex milites hortabitur. 7. Confiteor peccatum meum. 8. Frater ejus mortuus est. 9. Noli imitari malos. 10. Ubi est qui (*he who*) natus est rex Judaeorum? 11. Bene omnia fecit; et surdos fecit audire, et mutos loqui. 12. Oritur sol, et occĭdit.

13. Puella non mortua est, sed dormit. 14. Věni, sĕquĕre me. 15. Oves meae vocem meam audiunt : et ego cognosco eas, et sequuntur me. 16. Ortus est sol. 17. Christus pro nobis mortuus est. 18. Manducemus et bibamus ; cras enim moriemur. 19. Deum veneramur, qui nos creavit. 20. Nemo nascitur sapiens. 21. Ecce nos dimisimus omnia, et secuti sumus te. 22. In omni loco oculi Domini contemplantur bonos et malos.

23. Et audivi vocem de caelo, dicentem mihi ; Scribe : Beati mortui qui in Domino moriuntur. 24. Domine, si fuisses hīc, non esset mortuus frater meus. 25. Revertar in domum meam, unde exivi. 26. Eamus et (*also*) nos, ut moriamur cum eo. 27. Jesu, fili David, miserere mei. 28. Oblivisci me fecit Deus omnium laborum meorum, et domus patris mei. 29. Dixitque Dominus ad eum :

G

"Ingredĕre tu, et omnis domus tua, in arcam." 30.
Audite multa, pauca loquimini. 31. Mutus non loquitur,
surdus non audit, caecus non videt. 32. Magister discipulos hortari amat. 33. Peccata sua confessi sunt. 34.
Peccata sua confitebuntur.

35. O mi pater, miserēre mei. 36. O Deus, miserēre
nostri.[2] 37. O Deus, hominum cunctorum miserēre. 38.
Verentur parentes: regem timent. 39. Parentes meos
verebor. 40. Filium meum verebuntur. 41. Ortusne[3]
sol ? 42. Sol orietur. 43. Heri amicus meus mortuus
est. 44. O pueri ! veremini parentes. 45. Veremini
Deum. 46. Peccatum suum confessus est. 47. Sine
dentibus nati sumus. 48. Tollat crucem suam, et sequatur
me.

49. Melior est canis vivens leone mortuo.[4] 50. Quomodo
miseretur pater filiorum.[5] 51. Obliti sunt Domini Dei sui.[6]
52. Cum sacerdotio fungeretur.[7] 53. Ut fruatur parte
suā.[8] 54. Modico vino utere.[9] 55. Nisi panem quo vesceb-
atur.[10] 56. Lacrymatus est Jesus.[11] 57. Ingressus in
templum Domini.[12]

---

[1] See § 98. [2] *Nostri*, Gen. Plur. of *ego*. § 27. [3] See Ex. 12, note. [4] See §
90, c. [5] See § 98, a. [6] See § 98, c. [7] See § 122, a. [8] See § 122, b. [9] See §
122, c. [10] See § 122, d. [11] See § 129, a. [12] See § 142.

EXERCISE XXVII.

Impersonal Verbs. § 80.

Edo, ēdi, ēsum, ēdĕre, 3, *to eat.*	interdum, adv., *sometimes.*
ĕm-o, ĕm-i. emt-um and empt-um,	nam, conj., *for.*
ĕm-ĕre, 3, *to buy.*	negligenti-a, ae, 1, *f., carelessness.*
expedit, *it is expedient.*	plant-o, āvi, ātum, are, 1, *to plant.*
fact-um, i, 2, n., *a deed.*	quod, *what, that.*
Herodes, is, 3, *Herod.*	uxor, ōris, 3, *f., a wife.*

vendo, dĭdi, dĭtum, dĕre, 3, *to sell.*

1. Miseret nos hominis.[1] 2. Piget puerum negligentiae.
3. Miseret me amici mei. 4. Taedet me vitae meae.[2] 5.
Miseret me tui. 6. Pudet me facti. 7. Dicebat enim
Joannes Herodi: "Non licet tibi habēre uxorem fratris
tui."[3] 8. Juravit Dominus, et non poenitebit eum.[1] 9.

Non licet mihi quod volo facĕre? 10. Poenituit eum quod hominem fecisset in terrā. 11. Poenitet me fecisse eos. 12. Me miseret illius hominis.

13. Pudet te tuae negligentiae. 14. Oportet me hoc facĕre. 15. Edĕre oportet ut vivamus, non vivĕre ut edamus. 16. Interdum ningit. 17. Eamus domum, nam pluit, tonat, et fulgurat. 18. Nos miseret eorum. 19. Oportet nos adorare Deum. 20. Spiritus est Deus; et eos, qui adorant eum, in spiritu et veritate oportet adorare. 21. Quid me oportet facĕre? 22. Omnia mihi licent sed non omnia expediunt. 23. Expedit vobis ut ego vadam.[4] 24. Hic dicet tibi quid te oporteat facĕre.[5] 25. Edebant, et bibebant; emebant, et vendebant; plantabant, et aedificabant.[6]

[1] See § 99, b. [2] See § 99, c. [3] See § 105, a. [4] See § 105, b. [5] See § 102, b. [6] See § 131.

EXERCISE XXVIII.

Defective Verbs. § 79.

Argente-us, a, um, *made of silver.*	quóniam, conj., *for.*
Caesar, Caesăr-is, 3, *m.*, *Caesar.*	reddo, reddĭdi, reddĭtum, reddĕre,
et, conj., *also.*	*to render.*
Imăgo, imagĭn-is, 3, *f.*, *image.*	superscriptio, ŏnis, 3, *f.*, *super-*
Ismaelit-i, orum, 2, pl., *Ishmaelites.*	*scription.*
quia, conj., *that.*	

1. Ego odi eum. 2. Qui[1] me odit, et Patrem meum odit. 3. Domine, tu omnia nosti, tu scis quia amo te. 4. Et veniebant ad eum, et dicebant: "Ave, rex Judaeorum!" 5. Qui non diligit, non novit Deum, quoniam Deus caritas est. 6. Et ait illis Jesus: "Cujus est imago haec, et superscriptio?" 7. Dicunt ei, "Caesaris." Tunc ait illis, "Reddite ergo quae sunt Caesaris, Caesari; et quae sunt Dei, Deo." 8. Memento creatōris tui.[2] 9. Non sunt nobis, plus quam quinque panes.[3] 10. Quod tibi nomen est? Legio mihi nomen est.[4] 11. Vendiderunt eum Ismaelitis viginti argenteis.[5]

[1] *Qui*, he that. [2] See § 98, b. [3] See § 104, a. [4] See § 104, b, c. [5] See § 121.

EXERCISE XXIX.

Adverbs.   § 71.

Cělěrĭter, adv., *quickly.*
fŏris, adv., *out-of-doors.*

quōmŏdo, adv., *how.*
super, prep. with acc., *more than.*

1. Foris ambulemus. 2. Hodie epistolam scripsi. 3.
Bene vivĕre, bis vivĕre est : bene vivite. 4. Surdi non
audiunt. 5. Vĕni huc. 6. Ecce venio cito. 7. Multas a
te accēpi epistolas, omnes diligenter scriptas. 8. Eamus
in urbem iterum. 9. Tulerunt Dominum meum, et nescio
ubi posuerunt eum. 10. Ubi est ille ? 11. Jam non sum
dignus vocari filius tuus.

12. Manducabimus et bibemus, cras enim moriemur.
13. Domine, si fuisses hĩc, non esset mortuus frater meus.
14. Heri amicus meus mortuus est.   15. Revertar in
domum meam, unde exivi. 16. Qui amat patrem aut
matrem plus quam me, non est me dignus ;[1] et qui amat
filium aut filiam super me, non est me dignus. 17. Ecce
quomodo amaba[+] eum ! 18. Currit celeriter. 19. Currite
celeriter. 20. Milites fortissime pugnant. 21. Epistolae
sunt pessime[2] scriptae. 22. Facile est scribĕre; non facile
est bene scribĕre.

[1] See Rule, § 124. [2] *Pessime*, sup. adv., *very badly*, § 73.

EXERCISE XXX.

Prepositions.   § 75.

Apud, prep. with acc., *with.*
collĭg-o, collēg-i, collect-um, collĭg-ĕre, 3, *to gather.*
contra, prep. with acc., *against.*
disperg-o, dispers-i, dispers-um, disperg-ĕre, 3, *to scatter.*
emund-o, avi, atum, are, 1, *to cleanse.*
fieri, *to be made,* infin. of fio.
labi-um, 2, *n., a lip.*
longe, adv., *far.*

per, prep. with acc., *through.*
requiesc-o, requiēv-i, requiēt-um, requiesc-ĕre, 3, *to rest.*
sit, *let it be,* 3, sing. pres. subj. of sum, used as an imperative.
super, prep. with acc. or abl., *above, upon.*
turbāti sunt, *they were troubled,* 3. pl. perf. indic. pass. of turb-o, avi, atum, are, 1, *to trouble*
vigili-a, ae, 1, *f., a watch.*

1. In templo ambulabat. 2. Domos in urbe aedificav-
erunt. 3. Sanguis Jesu Christi emundat nos ab omni
peccato. 4. Vade in pace. 5. Pax vobiscum. 6. Deus
est super omnia et per omnia. 7. Apud me sunt filii mei.
8. Sine dentibus nati sumus. 9. Ecce věnit cum nubibus.
10. Sanguis ejus (sit) super nos et super filios nostros. 11.
Populus hic labiis me honorat ; cor autem eorum longe est
a me. 12. Pater, peccavi in coelum et coram te. 13. Per
urbem ambulat. 14. Jesus věnit ad eos ambulans super
mare. 15. Vado ad Patrem. 16. Milites in urbem currunt.
17. Nobiscum ambulant.

18. Et nunc vado ad eum qui misit me ; et nemo ex
vobis interrogat me : Quo vadis ? 19. Nihil in hoc
mundo fieri sine Deo potest.[1] 20. Qui non est mecum
contra me est ; et qui non colligit mecum dispergit.
21. Agricolae pascebant oves in montibus. 22. Veniesne
mecum ? 23. Veniat ad me. 24. Věni in hortum meum.
25. Magistri a discipulis amantur. 26. Quartā vigiliā
noctis, věnit ad eos ambulans super mare. 27. Et videntes
eum super mare ambulantem, turbati sunt. 28. Laudatur
ab his : culpatur ab illis. 29. Crucifixi sunt cum eo duo
latrones. 30. In domum Domini eamus. 31. Tulitque[2]
annulum de manu suā. 32. Nolite peccare in puerum.

[1] *Fieri potest*, can be done. [2] *Que*, and, joined on to the end of the word.

EXERCISE XXXI.

The Lord's Prayer.

Advěnío, věni, ventum, věnire, 4, *to come.*
cael-um, i, 2, *n.*, or, cael-i, orum, 2, *m.*, pl., *heaven.*
děbǐtor, ǒris, 3, *m.*, *a debtor.*
děbǐt-um, i, 2, *n.*, *a debt.*
dimitt-o, misi, missum, mittěre, 3, *to forgive.*
fiat, *be done*, 3, sing. subj. pres. of fio, used as the passive of facio, § 73.

induc-o, duxi, ductum, ducěre, 3, *to lead.*
lǐber-o, avi, atum, are, 1, *to deliver.*
mal-us, i, 2, *m.*, *the Evil One*, or, mal-um, i, 2, *n.*, *evil.*
quotǐdǐān-us, a, um, *daily.*
regn-um, i, 2, *n.*, *a kingdom.*
sanctǐfǐc-o, avi, atum, are, 1, *to hallow.*

Pater noster, qui es in caelis, sanctificetur[1] nomen tuum.
Adveniat regnum tuum. Fiat voluntas tua sicut in caelo
et in terrâ. Panem nostrum quotidianum da nobis hodie.
Et dimitte nobis[2] debita nostra, sicut et nos dimittimus
debitoribus nostris. Et ne[3] nos inducas in tentationem.
Sed libera nos a malo. AMEN.

[1] *Sanctificetur*—The Subjunctive is used to express a wish, see § 136.
[2] *Nobis*, a dative of advantage after *dimitte*. [3] § 137.

EXERCISE XXXII.

Visit of the Angel Gabriel to Zacharias.

Aaron, *of Aaron.*
a dextris, *on the right side.*
Abia, *of Abia.*
altāre, ris, 3, *n., an altar.*
ambo, *both.* § 25.
ante, prep. with acc., *before.*
appār-eo, ui, Itum, ēre, 2, *to appear.*
consuētūdo, dĭnis, 3, *f., custom.*
cum, adv., *when.*
de, prep. with abl., *of.*
dēprĕcātio, ōnis, 3, *f., prayer.*
Elisabeth, *Elizabeth.*
exaudīta est, *is heard*, 3, s. perf.
  indic. pass. from ex, and audio.
exsultātio, ōnis, 3, *f., gladness.*
fŏris, adv., *without, out of doors.*
fuit, *there was*, perf. of sum.
fungor, functus sum, fungi, 3, *to
  execute* (gov. abl). § 122.
gaudĕo, gāvīsus sum, gaudēre, 2,
  to rejoice.
gaudi-um, i, 2, *n., joy.*
Herod-es, is, 3, *Herod.*
incēdentes, *walking*, pres. part. pl.
  of incēd-o, incess-i, incess-um,
  incēd-ĕre, *to walk.*
incensum ponĕre, *to burn incense.*

ingress-us, *entered*, past part. of
  ĭngrĕdior, ingressus sum, ingrĕdi,
  to enter.
irru-o, ui, ĕre, 3, *to fall upon.*
Joann-es, is, 3, *John.*
Judaea, ae, 1, *Judea.*
justificatio, ōnis, 3, *f., ordinance.*
just-us, a, um, *just.*
mandāt-um, i, 2, *n., a commandment.*
nātivitas, ātis, 3, *f., birth.*
orans, ntis, *praying*, pres. part. of
  oro.
ordo, dĭnis, 3, *m., order.*
pări-o, pĕpĕri, part-um, parĕre, 3,
  to bear.
quĕrēla, ae, 1, *f., complaint.*
săcerdos, ōtis, 3, *m., a priest.*
săcerdōti-um, i, 2, *n., the priest's
  office.*
sors, sort-is, 3, *f., lot.*
tĭmor, ōris, 3, *m., fear.*
turbātus est, *was troubled*, perf.
  ind. pass. of turbo, *to trouble.*
vicis (Gen. has no Nominative), 3,
  f., a course.
de vice, *of the course.*
Zacharias, *Zacharias.*

Fuit in diebus Herodis, regis Judaeae,[1] sacerdos quidam
nomine Zacharias,[2] de vice Abia; et uxor illius de filiabus[3]
Aaron, et nomen ejus Elisabeth. Erant autem justi ambo
ante Deum, incedentes in omnibus mandatis et justifica-
tionibus Domini sine querela,[4] et non erat illis filius.[5]
Factum est[6] autem, cum sacerdotio fungeretur[7] in ordine
vicis suae ante Deum, secundum consuetudinem sacerdotii,
sorte exiit[8] ut incensum poneret,[9] ingressus in templum
Domini;[10] et omnis multitudo populi erat orans foris

horā incensi. Apparuit autem illi angelus Domini, stans a dextris altaris incensi. Et Zacharias turbatus est videns, et timor irruit super eum. Ait autem ad illum angelus. Ne timeas, Zacharia, quoniam exaudita est deprecatio tua, et uxor tua Elisabeth pariet tibi filium, et vocabis nomen ejus Joannem; et erit gaudium tibi,⁵ et exsultatio, et multi in nativitate ejus gaudebunt.—Luc. i.

¹ Rule, § 87. ² *Nomine Zacharias*—Zacharias by name; named Zacharias. ³ *Filiabus*: The Dative and Ablative Plural of some Feminine Nouns of the First Declension end in *abus*, to distinguish them from the Masculines of the Second Declension which make their Dative and Ablative Plural in *is*, such as—*dea*, a goddess, and *filia*, a daughter. The Feminines of *duo*, two, and *ambo*, both, make their Dative and Ablative Plural *duabus* and *ambabus*; see § 25. ⁴ *Sine querela*, blameless. ⁵ *Non erat illis filius*, they had no child; see § 104. ⁶ *Factum est*, it came to pass. ⁷ *Cum sacerdotio fungeretur*, when he executed the priest's office; see § 122, *a*. ⁸ *Sorte exiit*, his lot was; lit., he went out by lot. ⁹ *Ut incensum poneret*, to burn incense. ¹⁰ See § 141.

EXERCISE XXXIII.

Visit of the Angel Gabriel to the Virgin Mary.

Abi-it, = abivit, *went*, 8, s. perf. ind. of ab-eo.
altissim-us, a, um, sup. adj., *highest*.
ancill-a, ae, 1, *f.*, *handmaid*.
cīvitas, ātis, 3, *f.*, *a city*.
concǐpi-o, cēpi, ceptum, cǐpěre, 3, *to conceive*.
cogǐt-o, avi, atum, are, 1, *to cast in the mind*.
David, *of David*.
desponsāt-a, past part., *f.*, *espoused*.
discess-it, *departed*, 3, s. perf. indic. of discēd-o.
exsurg-o, rexi, rectum, ěre, 3, *to arise*.
festinatio, ōnis, 3, *f.*, *haste*.
fiat mihi, *be it unto me;* fiat, 3, s. subj. of fio, the passive of facio.
fīnis, is, 3, m., *end*.
Gabriel, *Gabriel*.
Galilaea, ae, *Galilee*.
grati-a, ae, 1, *f.*, *grace, favour*.

in aeternum, *for ever*.
intr-o, avi, atum, are, 1, *to enter*.
Jacob, *of Jacob*.
Joseph, *Joseph*.
Juda, *of Judah*.
Maria, *Mary*.
mensis, is, 3, m., *a month*.
missus est, *was sent*, 8, s. perf. indic. pass. of mitto.
montān-us, a, um, *hilly*.
in montāna, *into the hill country*.
Nazareth, *Nazareth*.
plēn-us, a, um, *full of*, followed by an abl. § 123.
quālis, e, *what manner of*.
regn-o, avi, atum, are, 1, *to reign*.
salutatio, ōnis, 3, *f.*, *salutation*.
salut-o, avi, atum, are, 1, *to salute*.
sēdes, is, 3, *f.*, *a seat*.
sermo, ōnis, 3, m., *saying*.
sext-us, a, um, *sixth*.
Zachariae, *of Zacharias*.

In mense autem sexto, missus est angelus Gabriel a Deǫ in civitatem Galilaeae, cui nomen¹ Nazareth, ad virginem desponsatam viro, cui nomen¹ erat Joseph, de domo David, et nomen virginis Maria. Et ingressus angelus ad eam dixit: "Ave, gratiā plena;² Dominus tecum;³ benedicta

tu in mulieribus !" Quae cum audisset, turbata est in
sermone ejus, et cogitabat qualis esset ista salutatio.⁴ Et
ait angelus ei : "Ne timeas, Maria, invenisti enim gratiam
apud Deum ; ecce concipies, et paries filium, et vocabis
nomen ejus JESUM. Hic erit magnus, et Filius Altissimi
vocabitur, et dabit illi Dominus Deus sedem David, patris
ejus ; et regnabit in domo Jacob in aeternum, et regni ejus
non erit finis." Dixit autem Maria: "Ecce ancilla Domini,
fiat mihi secundum verbum tuum." Et discessit ab illā
angelus. Exsurgens autem Maria in diebus illis abiit in
montana cum festinatione, in civitatem Juda ; et intravit
in domum Zachariae, et salutavit Elisabeth.—LUC. i.

---

[1] See § 104. [2] *Gratia plena*, full of grace ; otherwise translated—(thou
that art) highly favoured. [3] *Tecum*, with thee. The preposition *cum*,
with, is joined on to the end of the Relative, Personal, and Reflective
Pronouns. [4] See § 136, c.

EXERCISE XXXIV.
The Birth of Our Blessed Lord.

Ad invicem, *one to another.*
August-us, i, 2, *Augustus.*
Bethlehem, *Bethlehem.*
Caesar, *Caesar*, gen. Caesăr-is, dat.
  Caesăr-i, acc. Caesăr-em, abl.
  Caesăr-e.
circumfulg-eo, fulsi, fulgēre, 2, *to
  shine round about.*
clārĭta-, ātis, 3, *f., glory.*
cognōvērunt, *made known abroad,*
  3, pl. perf. indic. of cognosco.
conserv-o, avi, atum, are, 1, *to keep.*
custod-io, ivi, itum, ire, 4, *to keep ;*
  custodientes vigilias, *keeping
  watch.*
Cyrin-us, *Cyrenius.*
descrīb-o, scrips-i, script-um, scrīb-
  ĕre, 3, *to tax.*
descripti-o, ōnis, 3, *f., taxing.*
diversori-um, 2, *n., an inn.*
edict-um, 2, *n., a decree.*
eo quod, *because.*
evangeliz-o, avi, atum, are, 1, *I
  bring glad tidings.*
fămĭli-a, ae, 1, *f., lineage.*
festinantes, *with haste, lit., hasten-
  ing,* from festin-o, avi, atum, are,
  1, *to hasten.*
glorificantes, *glorifying*, pres. part.
  of glorific-o, avi, atum, are, 1,
  to glorify.

infans, ntis, 3, *c., an infant.*
involv-o, volv-i, volūt-um, volv-ĕre,
  3, *to wrap.*
juxta, prep. with acc., *near to.*
loc-us, i, 2. m., *room.*
militia caelestis, *the heavenly host.*
mir-or, ātus sum, āri, 1, dep., *to
  wonder.*
noct-is, *by night.*
ostend-o, ostend-i, ostens-um, and
  tum, ostend-ĕre, 3, *to make known.*
pann-us, i, 2, *m., a small cloth for
  binding with,* pann-i, orum, pl.
  swaddling-clothes.
po-it-us, a, um, *lying* or *placed,*
  from pōn-o, pŏs-ui, pŏsit-um,
  pōn-ĕre, 3, *to lay* or *place.*
praesepi-um, 2, *n., a manger.*
praeses, praesid is, 3, *m., governor.*
primogenit-us, a, um, *first-born.*
profit-eor, professus sum, profit-
  ēri, 2, *to be taxed.*
reclīn-o, avi, atum, are, 1, *to lay.*
regio, ōnis, 3, *f., a country.*
singul-i, orum (ae, arum), pl. *each.*
stětit, *came*, lit. *stood,* 3, a. perf. of
  sto.
subito, *suddenly.*
Syria, ae, *Syria.*
univers-us orb-is, *the whole world.*
usque, *even.*

Factum est autem in diebu- illis, exiit edictum a Caesare
Augusto, ut describeretur universus orbis. Haec descriptio
prima facta est a praeside Syriae Cyrino. Et ibant omnes,
ut profiterentur singuli in suam civitatem. Ascendit
autem et Joseph a Galilaeâ de civitate Nazareth, in
Judaeam, in civitatem David, quae vocatur Bethlehem ; eo
quod esset de domo et familiâ David, ut profiteretur cum
Mariâ. Factum est autem, cum essent ibi, peperit filium
suum primogenitum, et pannis eum involvit, et reclinavit
eum in praesepio, quia non erat eis locus in diversorio.

Et pastores erant in regione eâdem vigilantes, et custodientes vigilias noctis super gregem suum. Et ecce angelus
Domini stetit juxta illos, et claritas Dei circumfulsit illos,
et timuerunt timore magno. Et dixit illis angelus : "Nolite
timēre ; ecce enim evangelizo vobis gaudium magnum,
quod erit omni populo: quia natus est vobis hodie Salvator,
qui est Christus Dominus, in civitate David. Et hoc
vobis signum : Invenietis infantem pannis involutum, et
positum in praesepio." Et subito facta est cum angelo
multitudo militiae coelestis, laudantium Deum, et dicen-
tium : "Gloria in altissimis Deo, et in terrâ pax hominibus
bonae voluntatis." Et factum est, ut discesserunt ab eis
angeli in coelum, pastores loquebantur ad invicem :
"Transeamus usque Bethlehem, et videamus hoc verbum,[1]
quod factum est, quod Dominus ostendit nobis." Et
venerunt festinantes, et invenerunt Mariam, et Joseph et
infantem positum in praesepio. Videntes autem cognoverunt de verbo,[2] quod dictum erat illis de puero hoc. Et
omnes qui audierunt,[3] mirati sunt et de his quae dicta
erant a pastoribus ad ipsos. Maria autem conservabat
omnia verba haec, conferens in corde suo. Et reversi sunt
pastores glorificantes et laudantes Deum,[4] in omnibus
quae audierant[3] et viderant, sicut dictum est ad illos.—
Luc. ii., 1—20.

[1] *Hoc verbum*, this thing ; lit., this word. [2] *Cognoverunt de verbo*, they made known abroad the saying. [3] See § 60. [4] See § 140.

EXERCISE XXXV.

Christ raiseth Lazarus.

Bethani-a, *Bethany.*
capill-us, 1, 2, *m.*, *hair* (of the head).
castellum, 1, 2, *n.*, *town.*
cĕcidit, *fell down,* 3, sing. perf.
  indic. of cado.
circumsto, steti, statum, stare, *to
  stand around.*
condiscipul-us, 1, 2, *m.*, *fellow-
  disciple.*
consŏl-or, ătus sum, āri, 1, dep.,
  to comfort.
Didymus, *Didymus* (a word signifying. a twin).
dormiti-o, onis, 3, *f.*, *a sleeping.*
duodecim, *twelve.*
elev-o, avi, atum, are. 1, *to lift up.*
excit-o, avi, atum, are, 1, *to awake.*
exterg-eo, exters-i, exters-um, ex-
  terg-ēre, 2, *to wipe.*
faci-es, e , 5, *f.*, *a face.*
foet-eo, ēre, 2, *to stink.*
foras, adv., *forth.*
gaud-eo, gavis-us sum, gaud-ēre, 2,
  to be glad.
glori-a, 1, *f.*, *glory.*
glorific-o, avi, atum, are, 1, *to
  glorify.*
gratias ago, *I thank thee.*
illuc, adv., *thither.*
infirmitas, atis, 3, *f.*, *sickness.*
infirm-or, atus sum, ari, 1, *I am
  sick.*
infrem-o, ui, uĕre, 3, *to groan.*
instit-ae, arum, 1, *f.*, pl., *grave-
  clothes.*
juxta, prep. with acc., *nigh to.*
languens, *sick.*
lapid-o, avi, atum, are, 1, *to stone.*
Lazarus, *Lazarus.*
ligat-us, a, um, *bound*
manifeste, adv., *plainly.*
Martha, *Martha.*
mon ment-um, 1, 2, *n.*, *a grave,
  sepulchre.*
nondum, adv., *not yet.*

nunc, adv., *of late, just now.*
occurr-o, occurr-i, occursum, occur-
  rĕro (with a dative), *to meet.*
offend-o, offend-i, offens-um, offend-
  ĕre, 3, *to stumble.*
pĕs, pĕd-is, 3, *m.*, *a foot.*
Pharisae-i, orum, 2, *m.*, pl., *the
  Pharisees.*
posc-o, poposc-i, posc-ĕre, 3, *to ask.*
post, prep. with acc., *after.*
pro, prep. with abl., *for.*
prodiit, *came forth,* 3, s. perf. indic.
  of prodeo, ivi and ii, itum, ire.
propter, prep. with acc., *on account
  of,* propter vos, *for your sakes.*
put-o, avi, atum, are. 1, *to think.*
quaer-o, quaesiv-i, quaesit-um,
  quaer-ĕre, 3, *to seek.*
quasi, *about.*
quatriduan-us, a, um, *of four days.*
quindecim, *fifteen.*
Rabbi, *Master.*
resurrectio, ōnis, 3, *f.*, *the resurrec-
  tion.*
rursum, *again.*
salv-us, a, um, *well, in good health.*
sĕd-eo, sĕd-i, sessum, sĕd-ĕre, 2, *to
  sit.*
silentio, *secretly,* abl. sing. of silenti-
  um, 1, 2, *n.*, *silence.*
spĕlunc-a, ae, 1, *f.*, *a cave.*
stadi-um, 1, 2, *n.*, *a Grecian measure
  of distance; viz.—125 paces,* or *625
  feet.*
statim, *immediately.*
sudari-um, 2, *n.*, *a napkin.*
superpon-o, pos-ui, posit-um, ponĕre, 3, *to lay upon.*
surrexit, *rose up,* 3, sing. perf.
  indic. of surg-o.
sursum, *up.*
unguent-um, 2, *n.*, *ointment.*
ungu-o, unx-i, unct-um, ungu-ĕre,
  3, *to anoint.*
utique, *yea.*

Erat autem quidam languens Lazarus a Bethania, de
castello Mariae et Marthae, sororis ejus. (Maria autem
erat, quae unxit Dominum unguento, et extersit pedes ejus
capillis suis; cujus frater Lazarus infirmabatur.) Miserunt
ergo sorores ejus ad eum, dicentes: "Domine, ecce quem

amas infirmatur." Audiens autem Jesus dixit eis: "Infirmitas haec non est ad mortem, sed pro gloriâ Dei, ut
glorificetur Filius Dei per eam." Diligebat autem Jesus
Martham, et sororem ejus Mariam, et Lazarum. Post
haec dixit discipulis suis: "Eamus in Judaeam iterum."
Dicunt ei discipuli: "Rabbi, nunc quaerebaut te Judaei
lapidare, et iterum vadis illuc?" Respondit Jesus:
"Nonne duodecim sunt horae diei? Si quis ambulaverit[1]
in die, non offendit, quia lucem hujus mundi videt; si
autem ambulaverit[1] in nocte, offendit, quia lux non est in
eo." Haec ait, et post haec dixit eis: "Lazarus amicus
noster dormit; sed vado ut a somno excitem eum."
Dixerunt ergo discipuli ejus: "Domine, si dormit, salvus
erit.[2]" Dixerat autem Jesus de morte ejus; illi autem
putaverunt quia de dormitione somni[3] diceret. Tunc ergo
Jesus dixit eis manifeste: "Lazarus mortuus est; et
gaudeo propter vos, ut credatis, quoniam non eram ibi.
Sed eamus ad eum." Dixit ergo Thomas, qui dicitur
Didymus, ad condiscipulos: "Eamus et nos, ut moriamur
cum eo."

Vĕnit itaque Jesus, et invĕnit eum quatuor dies jam in
monumento habentem. (Erat autem Bethania juxta
Jerosolymam quasi stadiis quindecim.) Multi autem ex
Judaeis venerant ad Martham et Mariam, ut consolarentur
eas de fratre suo. Martha ergo ut audivit quia Jesus
vĕnit, occurrit illi; Maria autem domi[4] sedebat. Dixit
ergo Martha ad Jesum: "Domine, si fuisses hīc, frater
meus non fuisset mortuus. Sed et nunc scio quia quae-
cumque poposceris a Deo, dabit tibi Deus." Dicit illi
Jesus: "Resurget frater tuus."[5] Dicit ei Martha: "Scio
quia resurget in resurrectione in novissimo die." Dixit ei
Jesus: "Ego sum resurrectio et vita; qui credit in me,
etiam si mortuus fuerit, vivet; et omnis qui vivit et credit
in me, non morietur in aeternum. Credis hoc?" Ait illi:
"Utique, Domine, ego credidi quia tu es Christus, Filius

Dei vivi, qui in hunc mundum venisti." Et cum (*when*)
haec dixisset, abiit, et vocavit Mariam, sororem suam,[6]
silentio, dicens : "Magister adest, et vocat te." Illa ut
audivit, surgit cito, et vēnit ad eum. Nondum enim
venerat Jesus in castellum ; sed erat ad huc in illo loco,
ubi occurrerat ei Martha. Judaei ergo qui erant cum eā
in domo, et consolabantur eam, cum vidissent Mariam
quia cito surrexit et exiit, secuti sunt eam, dicentes :
"Quia vadit ad monumentum, ut ploret tibi." Maria ergo,
cum venisset ubi erat Jesus, videns eum, cĕcĭdit ad pedes
ejus, et dicit ei : "Domine, si fuisses hĭc, non esset
mortuus frater meus." Jesus ergo, ut vidit eam plor-
antem, et Judaeos, qui venerant cum eā, plorantes,
infremuit spiritu, et turbavit seipsum, et dixit : "Ubi
posuistis eum?"[7] Dicunt ei : "Domine, vēni, et vide."
Et lacrymatus est Jesus.[8] Dixerunt ergo Judaei : "Ecce
quomodo amabat eum." Quidam autem ex ipsis dixerunt :
"Non poterat hic, qui aperuit oculos caeci nati, facĕre ut
hic non moreretur?" Jesus ergo rursum fremens in
semetipso,[9] vĕnit ad monumentum : erat autem spelunca,
et lapis superpositus erat ei. Ait Jesus : "Tollite
lapidem."[10] Dicit ei Martha, soror ejus qui mortuus
fuerat : "Domine, jam foetet, quatriduanus est enim."
Dicit ei Jesus : "Nonne dixi tibi quoniam si credideris,
videbis gloriam Dei." Tulerunt ergo lapidem ; Jesus
autem elevatis sursum oculis,[11] dixit : "Pater, gratias ago
tibi quoniam audisti me. Ego autem sciebam quia semper
me audis ; sed propter populum, qui circumstat, dixi, ut
credant quia tu me misisti." Haec cum dixisset, voce
magnā clamavit : "Lazare, vĕni foras." Et statim prodiit
qui fuerat mortuus, ligatus pedes et manūs institis, et
facies illĭus sudario erat ligata. Dixit eis Jesus : "Solvite
eum, et sinite abire."[12]

Multi ergo ex Judaeis, qui venerant ad Mariam et
Martham, et viderant quae fecit Jesus, crediderunt in eum.

Quidam autem ex ipsis abiērunt ad Pharisaeos, et dixerunt eis quae fecit Jesus.—JOAN. xi.

 [1] See § 135. [2] *Salvus erit*, he shall do well. [3] *De dormitione somni*, of taking rest in sleep. [4] *Domi*, in the house, at home; see § 16, note. [5] See § 134. [6] See § 87. [7] See § 129, *b*. [8] See § 129, *a*. [9] *In se-met-ipso*, in Himself. The suffix—*met*—is added to various Pronouns to strengthen their meaning. [10] See § 138, *a*. [11] An Ablative Ab olute; see § 126, *a*. [12] See § 139.

EXERCISE XXXVI.

The Parable of the Wicked Husbandmen.

Apprehend-o, di, sum, ĕre, 8, *to take.*

appropinqu-o, avi, atum, are, 1, *to draw near.*

caed-o, cĕcīd-i, caes-um, caed-ĕre, 3, *to beat.*

circumd-o, dĕd-i, dăt-um, d-ăre, *to put around.*

ejic-io, ejēc-i, eject-um, ejic-ĕre, 8, *to cast out.*

extra, prep. with acc., *out of.*

fōdit, *digged*, 3, sing. perf. indic. of fōdio.

intra, prep. with acc., *among, within.*

loc-o, avi, atum, are, 1, *to let* or *hire out.*

male, adv., *wickedly, wretchedly.*

novissime, superl. adv., from nove, *last of all.*

paterfamilias, *a householder* (Gen., patrisfamilias; Dat., patrifa-milias, &c.).

perd-o, ĭdi, ĭtum, ĕre, 8, *to destroy.*

pĕrĕgre, adv., *into a far country.*

plant-o, avi, atum, āre, 1, *to plant.*

plus, plur-is, *more.*

prior, prior-is, *the first.*

profectus est, *went, set out*, 3, s. perf. of proficiscor.

redd-o, ĭdi, ĭtum, ĕre, *to render.*

sĕp-es, is, 3, *f.*, *a hedge.*

temp-us, ŏris, 3, *n.*, *season.*

torcŭlar, ăris, 3, *n.*, *a wine-press.*

turr-is, is, 3, *f.*, *a tower* (acc., im).

ver-eor, ĭtus sum, ēri, 2, dep., *to reverence.*

vero, *and.*

vine-a, ae, 1, *f.*, *a vineyard.*

Homo erat paterfamilias, qui plantavit vineam, et sepem circumdedit ei, et fōdit in eā torcular, et aedificavit turrim, et locavit eam agricolis, et peregre profectus est. Cum autem tempus fructuum appropinquasset,[1] misit servos suos ad agricolas, ut acciperent fructūs ejus. Et agricolae, apprehensis servis ejus,[2] alium cecīdĕrunt, alium occiderunt, alium vero lapidāvērunt. Iterum misit alios servos plures prioribus,[3] et fecerunt illis similiter. Novissime autem misit ad eos filium suum dicens: "Verebuntur filium meum." Agricolae autem videntes filium,[4] dixerunt intra se : "Hic est heres; venite, occidamus eum, et habebimus hereditatem ejus." Et apprehensum eum[5] ejecerunt extra vineam, et occiderunt. Cum ergo venerit[6] dominus vineae, quid faciet agricolis illis? Aiunt illi: "Malos male perdet,[7] et vineam suam locabit aliis agricolis, qui reddant ei fructum temporibus suis."—MATT. xxi., 33—41.

[1] *Appropinquasset* = *appropinquavisset;* see § 60. [2] *Apprehensis servis ejus,* took his servants. An Abl. Abs.; see § 126, a. [3] *Plures prioribus,* more than the first; see § 125. [4] *Agricolae autem videntes filium,* but when the husbandmen saw the son; see § 141. [5] *Et apprehensum eum,* and they caught him; see § 141. [6] *Venerit,* fut. perf. of venio, to be translated by an English present; see § 135. [7] *Malos male perdet,* he will miserably destroy (those) wicked men.

EXERCISE XXXVII.

Joseph's Two Dreams.

Ador-o, avi, atum, are, 1, *to make obeisance to.*
consider-o, avi, atum, are, 1, *to observe.*
consurg-o, rex-i, rect-um, surg-ĕre, 3, *to rise.*
dit-io, ōnis, 3, *f., dominion.*
eo quod, *because.*
genuisset, *had begotten,* 3, sing. plup. subj. of gign-o, gen-ui, gen-itum, gign-ĕre, 3, *to beget.*
increp-o, avi, atum, are, 1, *to rebuke.*
Israel, *Israel.*
lig-o, avi, atum, are, 1, *to bind.*
lun-a, ae, 1, *f., the moon.*
manipul-us, i, 2, *m., a sheaf.*
narr-o, avi, atum, are, 1, *to relate.*

numquid, used in asking a question when the answer "no" is expected.
pacifice, adv., *peaceably.*
pŏlymit-us, a, um, *of many colours.*
res, rei, 5, *f., a thing, the saying.*
retulisset, *had told,* 3, sing. plup. subj. of rĕfĕr-o, tŭli, lātum, ferre, *to relate, report.*
senect-us, ūtis, 3, *f., old age.*
somni-um, 2, *n., a dream;* somnium vidĕre, *to dream a dream.*
stell-a, 1, *f., a star.*
subjic-io, jĕci, jectum, jicĕre, 3, *to put under.*
tacitus, *in silence.*
tunic-a, 1, *f., a coat.*
undecim, *eleven.*
vero, conj., *but.*

Israel autem diligebat Joseph super omnes filios suos, eo quod in senectute genuisset eum; fecitque ei tunicam polymitam. Videntes autem fratres ejus quod a patre plus cunctis filiis amaretur, oderant[1] eum, nec poterant ei quidquam pacifice loqui.[2]

Dixitque ad eos: "Audite somnium meum quod vidi: Putabam nos ligare[3] manipulos in agro, et quasi consurgĕre manipulum meum, et stare, vestrosque manipulos circumstantes adorare manipulum meum." Responderunt fratres ejus : "Numquid rex noster eris ?[4] aut subjiciemur ditioni tuae ?"[5]

Aliud quoque vidit somnium, quod narrans fratribus, ait : "Vidi per somnium, quasi solem et lunam et stellas undecim adorare me."[3] Quod cum patri suo et fratribus retulisset, increpavit eum pater suus, et dixit : " Quid sibi vult hoc somnium quod vidisti ?[6] num ego et mater tua et fratres tui adorabimus te super terram ?"

Invidebant ei[7] igitur fratres sui pater vero rem tacitus considerabat.[8]—GEN. xxxvii.

---

[1] *Oderant eum*, they hated him ; see § 79, 5. [2] *Nec poterant ei quidquam pacifice loqui*, and could not speak peaceably unto him. [3] Accusative with Infinitive ; see § 112. [4] *Numquid rex noster eris ?* Shalt thou be our king ? or, Shalt thou indeed reign over us ? [5] *Subjiciemur ditioni tuae ?* Shall we be subjected to thy dominion ? or, Shalt thou indeed reign over us ? [6] *Quid sibi vult hoc somnium quod vidisti ?* What is this dream that thou hast dreamed ? [7] See § 102, *k*. [8] *Pater vero rem tacitus considerabat*, but his father observed the saying in silence.

EXERCISE XXXVIII.

Jacob sendeth Joseph to visit his brethren, who conspire his death.

Anim-a, ae, 1, *f., life, the soul.*
antequam, adv., *before.*
appar-eo, ui itum, ēre, 2, *to appear.*
at, conj., *and.*
cistern-a, ae, 1, *f., a pit.*
cogit-o, avi, atum, are, 1, *to conspire.*
devor-o, avi, atum, are, 1, *to devour.*
in Dothain, *to Dothan.*
effund-o, effūd-i, effūs-um, effund-ēre, 8, *to shed.*
erga, prep. with acc., *with.*
erip-io, erip-ui, erept-um, erip-ēre, 8, *to rid, deliver.*
err-o, avi, atum, are, 1, *to wander.*
fer-a, ae, 1, *f., a wild animal ;* fera pessima, *an evil beast.*
Hebren, *Hebron.*
indic-o, avi, atum, are, 1, *to tell.*
innoxi-us, a, um, *free from guilt.*
interfic-io, fēci, fect-um, fic-ēre, 8, *to destroy, kill.*
liber-o, avi, atum, are, 1, *to deliver.*
mutuo, *one to another.*
mor-or, atus sum, ari, 1, dep., *to tarry.*

nit-or, nixus sum, 8, *to strive.*
pec-us, ŏris, 3, *n., a flock.*
perg-o, perrex-i, perrect-um, perg-ēre, 8, *to go.*
praesto. adv., *here, ready.*
procul, adv., *afar off.*
projic-io, jēc-i, ject-um, jicēre, 8, *to cast.*
prosper-a, 2, *n.,* pl., *prosperity, good fortune.*
prōsum, prōfui, prōdesse, *to profit, to benefit ;* see § 41, Obs.
reced-o, cess-i, cess-um, ced-ēre, 8, *to depart.*
reddĕre, *to deliver ;* see also Vocab. to Ex xxxvi.
renunti-o, avi, atum, are, 1, *to bring word again.*
Ruben, *Reuben.*
serv-o, avi, atum, are, 1, *to preserve, keep.*
Sichem, *Shechem.*
solitud-o, inis, 3, *f., a wilderness.*
vall-is, is, 3, *f., a vale.*
vet-us, vet-eris, *old.*

Cumque fratres illius in pascendis gregibus patris morarentur in Sichem, Dixit ad eum Israel: "Fratres tui pascunt oves in Sichimis; vĕni, mittam te ad eos." Quo respondente,[1] "Praesto sum," ait ei: "Vade, et vide si cuncta prospera sint erga fratres tuos, et pecŏra;[2] et renuntia mihi quid agatur."[3]

Missus[4] de valle Hebron, vēnit in Sichem; invenitque eum vir errantem in agro, et interrogavit quid quaereret. At ille respondit: "Fratres meos quaero; indica mihi ubi pascant greges." Dixitque ei vir: "Recesserunt de loco isto; audivi autem eos dicentes: 'Eamus in Dothain.'" Perrexit ergo Joseph post fratres suos, et invēnit eos in Dothain.

Qui cum vidissent eum procul, antequam accederet ad eos, cogitaverunt illum occidĕre; et mutuo loquebantur: "Ecce somniator vĕnit; venite, occidamus eum, et mittamus in cisternam veterem, dicemusque: Fera pessima devoravit eum; et tunc apparebit quid illi prosint somnia sua.[5]" Audiens autem hoc Ruben, nitebatur liberare eum de manibus eorum, et dicebat: "Non interficiatis animam ejus, nec effundatis sanguinem; sed projicite eum in cisternam hanc, quae est in solitudine, manūsque vestras servate innoxias." Hoc autem dicebat, volens eripere eum de manibus eorum, et reddĕre patri suo.

---

[1] *Quo respondente*, an Ablative Absolute; see § 126.　[2] *Vide si cuncta prospera sint erga fratres tuos, et pecora*, see whether it be well with thy brethren, and (their) flocks.　[3] *Et renuntia mihi quid agatur*, and bring me word again.　[4] *Missus*, he sent him; literally, sent. See § 141. [5] *Quid illi prosint somnia sua*, what will become of his dreams.

PART III.—EXERCISES.

THE VULGATE LATIN COURSE.

Part III.—EXERCISES.

N.B.—For the Latin words required in the following exercises consult the Vocabularies of the corresponding exercises in Part II.

Words placed within brackets are not to be translated.

EXERCISE I.

1. Good fathers.[1] 2. Good mothers. 3. A good man.
4. A bad mother. 5. Good brothers. 6. A deceitful
brother. 7. Foolish mothers. 8. Foolish men.

9. Sacred temples. 10. Good shepherds. 11. A beloved
daughter. 12. All men. 13. All temples. 14. All sacred
temples. 15. A high wall. 16. A short law.

[1] Adjectives are generally placed after the Nouns they qualify.

EXERCISE II.

1. Long letters. 2. A good book. 3. Large books.
4. Many tables. 5. Many long tables. 6. Many long
walls. 7. A good girl. 8. All good women. 9. Good
works. 10. All good works. 11. A high mountain. 12.
A black horse.

13. All eyes. 14. All places. 15. All false witnesses.
16. Many angels. 17. Every angel. 18. Every law. 19.
All good laws. 20. A short way. 21. A powerful king.
22. Good daughters. 23. All brave soldiers. 24. Beloved
sons.

EXERCISE III.

1. Very high mountains. 2. Most learned men. 3.
Very useful books. 4. A very high wall. 5. Higher walls.
6. Longer letters. 7. Longer wars. 8. The best men.
9. The most powerful kings. 10. A most wretched mother.
11. A most unhappy woman. 12. A longer way.

13. The bravest soldiers. 14. The longest tables. 15.
A most beautiful woman. 16. The longest wars. 17.
Many beautiful animals. 18. All the most beautiful
animals. 19. All the black horses. 20. Many very long
tables. 21. Many high trees. 22. All the highest trees.
23. Many unhappy women. 24. A very learned man.

EXERCISE IV.

1. One man. 2. One woman. 3. One body. 4. Two
masters. 5. Two names. 6. Two nights. 7. The third
boy. 8. Seven tables. 9. The tenth table. 10. Five
boys. 11. Two girls. 12. The sixth man.

13. Two angels. 14. The fourth woman. 15. The
fifteenth part. 16. The second table. 17. Two bodies.
18. Five animals. 19. Four thousand. 20. Two thousand.
21. The fifth day. 22. The second day. 23. The seventh
day. 24. Two scribes.

EXERCISE V.

1. Our father.[1] 2. Our mother. 3. Our friends. 4. His book. 5. My voice. 6. My daughters. 7. My sons. 8. These gifts.[2] 9. My brother. 10. This brave soldier. 11. This long table. 12. All these men. 13. Thy gifts.

14. My masters. 15. Each woman. 16. Certain women. 17. All thy words. 18. All thy works. 19. Your reward. 20. Our bodies. 21. Your gifts. 22. Our God. 23. Our hope. 24. Our houses. 25. Certain men. 26. My long letters. 27. These cities. 28. All my letters. 29. My voice.

[1] Possessive Pronouns generally follow the Nouns to which they belong
[2] Demonstrative Pronouns stand before the Nouns they point out, as in English.

EXERCISE VI.

1. The fear of man.[1] 2. The sons of men. 3. The eyes of lords. 4. The eyes of masters. 5. The brothers of the lord. 6. The boy's brother.[2] 7. Flocks of lambs. 8. My friend's eyes. 9. The hands of men. 10. My hand. 11. The master's book. 12. The girl's books. 13. The master's lambs. 14. The king's garden. 15. The son's friend. 16. Men's eyes. 17. Men's voices.

18. The man's daughter. 19. The master's voice. 20. Five thousand men.[3] 21. Seven thousand boys. 22. The king's house.[4] 23. This man's son. 24. This boy's book. 25. Horses' eyes. 26. The girl's letter. 27. The master's life. 28. The gates of the city. 29. Men's hands. 30. These men's horses. 31. Each girl's voice. 32. The third part of the city.

[1] The Genitive usually follows the Noun it depends upon. [2] See Gram. § 8 (2). [3] See § 25 (3). [4] See § 16.

EXERCISE VII.

1. (We) are men.[1]   2. The kings are good.   3. The way is short.   4. (Ye) are shepherds.   5. Laws are good.   6. (We) are not shepherds.   7. God is good.   8. The Saviour is the light of the world.   9. (Ye) are mortal.   10. My father is a shepherd.   11. God is my hope.   12. (We) are mortal.   13. Thou art the King of the Jews.   14. This is my beloved Son.   15. (We) are boys.

[1] See §§ 90, 94.

EXERCISE VIII.

1. Christ is the Son of God.   2. Where is my son?   3. (We) are the sons of a husbandman.   4. (We) are not spies.   5. (I) am not a spy.   6. The temples are splendid.   7. The wicked are not happy.   8. (We) have been diligent.   9. Books are useful.   10. The way is short.   11. This life is short.   12. Where is thy father?   13. The soldiers will be brave.

EXERCISE IX.

1. The father loves (his) sons.[1]   2. Husbandmen plough.   3. The husbandman was ploughing.   4. Birds fly.   5. We love God.   6. They call us.   7. (They) build houses.   8. The boys were swearing.   9. Masters praise good boys.   10. Masters do not praise bad boys.   11. The boys pray.   12. He praises God.

13. They praise the Lord.   14. The master loves him.   15. The husbandman cries-out.   16. The girl was singing.   17. The virgins were singing.   18. The girls cry-out.   19. Fathers praise (their) sons.   20. Mothers praise (their)

daughters. 21. The father gives books to the boys. 22.
The husbandmen give houses to (their) sons. 23. The
king enters the city. 24. The birds sing upon the
trees.[2]

25. Sailors do not build houses. 26. Husbandmen do
not fight. 27. The sailors give birds to the virgins. 28.
Soldiers do not plough the fields. 29. The sailors were
singing. 30. The soldiers sing. 31. (We) plough the
fields. 32. (We) give books to the masters. 33. (We)
were walking in the garden. 34. The father loves (his)
daughter. 35. The daughters love (their) father. 36.
The brothers build houses. 37. The boys used-to-swear.[3]
38. The virgin prays. 39. The father calls his son. 40.
I do not love thee.

[1] In translating simple sentences, place the Latin words in the following order:—1. The Nominative with the words dependent on it. 2. The
Accusative. 3. The Verb; as, *Pater meus filias amat*, my father loves (his)
daughters. [2] See § 119. [3] The Imperfect Tense is used when we wish to
speak of an habitual action, or what was wont to be done; see § 131.

EXERCISE X.

1. (They) have built houses. 2. (They) will love us.
3. The girls will walk through the city.[1] 4. (We) have
called the boys. 5. The foolish (men)[2] have built houses
upon the sand. 6. The husbandmen will swear. 7. (We)
have sinned. 8. The father will give books to (his) sons.
9. Who calls me? 10. Who called us? 11. (I) shall give
the book to the boy. 12. The soldiers have entered the
city. 13. (We) had walked through the city.

14. (We) hoped. 15. The son had sinned. 16. (They)
had sinned. 17. The father himself will love us. 18
The foolish (men) had hoped. 19. Foolish (men) will

build houses. 20. The virgin will sing. 21. The husbandmen will plough. 22. The Lord will love His people. 23.
The foolish daughters had sinned. 24. The husbandmen
will have walked through the fields.

[1] *Per*, through, governs the Accusative ; see § 75. [2] See § 128.

EXERCISE XI.

1. Let the boys pray. 2. Let (them) love God. 3.
(They) would have built houses. 4. Let us love (our)
masters. 5. About to pray. 6. Let us walk through the
city. 7. Let all (men) honour the Lord. 8. Let him watch
and pray for us. 9. Watching and praying (*sing.*). 10.
Soldiers fighting. 11. Husbandmen ploughing. 12. Boys
walking. 13. Girls singing.

14. Let us pray without ceasing. 15. Boys ploughing
fields. 16. Brothers praying for us. 17. Of praying. 18.
Of walking. 19. By praying. 20. Let us hope. 21. Let
us give books to the girls. 22. Love (thou) the good
(*masc. plur.*). 23. Let the daughters sing.

24. The virgins may sing. 25. The wind might blow.
26. The winds might blow. 27. Call (thou) the boys. 28.
To love good (things).[1] 29. To have loved good (men).
30. I might have loved. 31. By loving. 32. Let the boys
love (their) teachers. 33. O, my friends, love the Lord !
34. Let them praise the name of the Lord. 35. Praise
(ye) the Lord. 36. It is a good (thing)[2] to praise the name
of the Lord.

[1] Neuter plural of *bonus, a, um—bona*, good things. [2] *Bonum est*, it is
good thing. § 128.

EXERCISE XII.

1. The master sees. 2. God sees you. 3. The masters see. 4. The boy has a book. 5. The boys have books. 6. The father was teaching (his) daughters. 7. They-who have the Son of God have life : they-who have not the Son of God have not life. 8. They-who fear God do not fear man. 9. (We) have a father and a mother. 10. (We) see the poor. 11. Blessed are all they that fear God.

12. How many books have (you)? Two. 13. How many birds do (you) see? Fourteen, and three foxes. 14. The boys have birds. 15. The masters have books. 16. Books teach us. 17. God sees me. 18. The birds fly. 19. Masters teach boys. 20. The bird has a nest. 21. The blind (man) does not see. 22. Bad (men) fear death. 23. Bad boys fear (their) masters. 24. Dost thou fear the master? 25. Jesus was teaching the people.

EXERCISE XIII.

1. The father has taught (his) daughters. 2. The mother had warned (her) son. 3. The teacher has advised the boy. 4. We saw you (*plur.*). 5. (They) have seen. 6. (We) saw the boy under a tree. 7. (They) saw lions under the trees. 8. God will see us. 9. (We) shall see my father. 10. (They) had seen the Lord. 11. The king has seen the city. 12. The lion has not hurt the man. 13. (I) shall remain there (for) two days.

EXERCISE XIV.

1. Fear (ye) God. 2. Let us fear the Lord. 3. O, master, teach these boys! 4. O, mother, teach these girls! 5. O, masters, teach us! 6. (We) are mortal; therefore we ought to fear death. 7. Boy, fill the water-pot with water.

8. Let the women fill the waterpots with water. 9. Fear (ye) the Lord, my sons, and the king. 10. The masters would have taught these boys. 11. The good mothers will have advised (their) daughters. 12. Let the boy have this book. 13. They fear men, let them fear the Lord. 14. They ought to fear God. 15. To teach boys. 16. To have taught girls.

———

EXERCISE XV.

1. The boys read. 2. The girls write. 3. (We) run. 4. The boys were running. 5. The two sisters are playing. 6. The boy learns. 7. The horses were running. 8. He is reading a letter. 9. The boy is feeding sheep. 10. Kings drink wine. 11. The girls used-to-drink water. 12. (Ye) write letters.

13. (They) neither write nor read. 14. Who writes this letter? 15. Husbandmen feed sheep and oxen. 16. The masters say. 17. The masters used-to-say.[1] 18. The boys run into the city. 19. The boy loves his sister. 20. My father feeds sheep upon the mountains.[2] 21. We drink wine : ye drink water.[3] 22. The husbandmen were-feeding sheep upon the mountains. 23. The horses were-running through the fields. 24. The king sends a scribe.

---

[1] Used to say, *dicebant;* see § 131. [2] Upon the mountains, *in montibus;* see § 75. [3] See § 98.

EXERCISE XVI.

1. We have read thy letters. 2. (We) said. 3. The boy has written a letter. 4. The girls have written letters. 5. (I) shall rise-again. 6. (They) will rise-again. 7. The father led (his) daughter into the city. 8. The husband-men will feed (their) sheep and oxen upon the mountains. 9. The shepherds were feeding (their) flocks. 10. What shall the boys eat? 11. What shall the girls drink?

12. Who wrote these letters? 13. Boys will learn. 14. The shepherd has written a letter (with) his-own hand. 15. (I) have read these books. 16. The pupils will read this book. 17. The boy has said. 18. The pupils have written letters to-day. 19. (We) have read the letters which you wrote. 20. (I) had drunk water. 21. The husbandmen will not drink wine.

EXERCISE XVII.

1. Read (ye) these books. 2. Let them read. 3. Let them write. 4. Let us read good books. 5. Let us write long letters. 6. Feed (ye) my sheep. 7. Let them feed my lambs. 8. Give me a letter. 9. Let us love (our) enemies. 10. Let us honour all men; let us love the brotherhood; let us fear God; and let us honour the king. 11. What he has seen the scribe has written in a book. 12. They-all desired to see me.

13. To live well is to live twice : let us live well. 14. (We) love to read good books. 15. It is not easy to read. 16. It is not easy to plough a field. 17. It is not easy to write a long letter. 18. (He) learns by teaching. 19. Boys do not learn by playing. 20. The boys read, that they may learn. 21. Let the boys read, that they may learn. 22. Give me this book. 23. The master teaches the boys that they may learn to read this book.

EXERCISE XVIII.

1. The boys sleep. 2. (We) come. 3. Who has come? 4. The boys hear. 5. (I) shall hear. 6. The husbandmen were sleeping. 7. In the fifth year. 8. In the sixth year. 9. (He) came, (he) saw, (he) conquered. 10. (We) came, (we) saw, (we) conquered. 11. (We) shall come, (we) shall see, (we) shall conquer.

12. Does he hear? 13. The master heard a voice. 14. The girls come. 15. Death will come. 16. Death has come. 17. The sheep hear the voice of the husbandman. 18. The sheep will hear the shepherd's voice. 19. The soldiers came into the city. 20. The king used-to-come into the garden. 21. The master punishes bad boys.

22. (We) praise the good (boys), (we) punish the bad. 23. (We) used-to-sleep. 24. (I) shall come to you (*sing.*). 25. The deaf (man) does not hear. 26. (We) hear the Lord. 27. The father will bury his son to-day. 28. (We) shall feel the heat of the sun to-day. 29. The king has buried his daughter to-day. 30. In the second month, on the second day of the month. 31. In the third month, on the tenth day of the month.

———

EXERCISE XIX.

1. Let the boys come. 2. (We) desire to come to you (*sing.*). 3. Come (ye) into my garden. 4. Let the boy open the gate. 5. James would have opened the gate. 6. I should have come to you (*sing.*). 7. Open (ye) the book. 8. O boys, come hither. 9. Let the pupils come into the master's garden.

EXERCISE XX.

1. The field will be ploughed. 2. The masters will always be loved by (their) pupils.[1] 3. We are never praised : you are often praised (*plur.*). 4. The man will be judged. 5. Fathers are loved by (their) sons. 6. The wicked will be punished : the good will be praised. 7. The field is ploughed. 8. The fields have been ploughed.[2] 9. Good boys are praised : bad boys are blamed.

10. The girl was praised (*perf.*) by (her) mother. 11. Houses have been built. 12. A good master will always be loved by (his) pupils. 13. The masters are loved. 14. Good (people) are loved by good (men). 15. The times will be changed : and we shall be changed in them. 16. We are praised by good (men) : we are blamed by the wicked. 17. The men may be judged. 18. He is blamed by this (man) : he is praised by that (man).

[1] When the *person by whom* is to be expressed, the preposition *a* or *ab* must be used. [2] See § 90.

EXERCISE XXI.

1. The boy is taught by a diligent master. 2. Let the boy be carefully taught. 3. Thou wast taught by the master. 4. The wicked will be feared ; the good will be loved. 5. The good are not feared. 6. The daughters are taught by (their) mother ; the sons by (their) father. 7. The pupils had been carefully taught. 8. The pupils have been advised. 9. The girls will be frightened. 10. The boys are not frightened.

EXERCISE XXII.

1. Good books are read. 2. Letters will be sent. 3. These books will be read by all boys. 4. Let the thieves be crucified. 5. Pilate crucified the two thieves. 6. The two thieves were crucified by Pilate. 7. A letter has been written. 8. A letter had been sent. 9. He was sent by the king. 10. The girl was led to (her) mother. 11. The soldiers have been conquered. 12. Letters will be sent.

EXERCISE XXIII.

1. (We) are heard. 2. The girls are clothed. 3. The boys and girls will be clothed. 4. These pupils have been carefully instructed. 5. Let the wicked (man) be punished. 6. The bodies had been buried. 7. These boys have been punished by the master. 8. Wicked men are punished by God. 9. Let these bodies be buried. 10. Voices are heard. 11. A voice was heard (*perf.*). 12. Voices had been heard.

EXERCISE XXIV.

1. God made all things. 2. What shall we do? 3. The birds make (their) nests. 4. What has (he) done? 5. The enemy (*pl.*) will flee. 6. The husbandman will dig. 7. (We) have received letters. 8. (We) shall receive many letters. 9. God made the earth. 10. (They) will receive many other things. 11. To receive letters. 12. To have received many letters.

EXERCISE XXV.

1. (We) cannot read. 2. This husbandman can plough. 3. (We) cannot understand. 4. (They) cannot write. 5. Can (they) plough? 6. Can (you, *sing.*) read? 7. Masters wish to be loved. 8. (We) do not wish to live. 9. Let (us) go into the city. 10. Can (they) teach? 11. (They) cannot dig. 12. Little girls cannot close the gates. 13. The husbandman wished (*imperf.*) to sleep.

14. The masters are always present. 15. Boys become learned by learning.[1] 16. They are coming to close the gates.[2] 17. They came to close the gates.[3] 18. They have come to close the gates.[4] 19. Let them come that they may close the gates. 20. They had come that they might close the gates. 21. The boys have gone into the city. 22. O, husbandmen, take the stones away. 23. He has taken the stones away. 24. Go home, boys; we will remain. 25. O, boys, do not drink wine![5] 26. That the boys may become learned.[6]

[1] Learned, *docti;* by learning, *discendo.* [2] *Say,* that they may close the gates; see Sentences 16—20, in Latin Exercise xxv. [3] *Say,* that they might close. [4] *Say,* that they may close. [5] Not, with the Imperative, is translated by *ne: Ne bibite,* do not drink. [6] See § 94.

————

EXERCISE XXVI.

1. We exhort the men. 2. (He) exhorted (his) son. 3. The king exhorted the soldiers. 4. To pity the man (*gen.*).[1] 5. To exhort men. 6. To imitate the wicked. 7. (They) have done all (things) well. 8. (We) will follow thee. 9. Let them eat and drink. 10. All (men) will die. 11. (We) will return into the city. 12. Deaf (men) do not hear; blind (men) do not see; dumb (men) do not speak;

13. The dumb cannot speak.[2] 14. The masters exhort (their) pupils. 15. We reverence (our) parents. 16. The boy died yesterday. 17. The parents of this boy died yesterday.

[1] See § 98. [2] Say, the dumb are not able to speak ; non possunt.

EXERCISE XXVII.

1. He pities the man.[1] 2. He is weary of life.[2] 3. I pity this boy.[3] 4. He pities me. 5. He will be ashamed of the deed.[4] 6. Let him be ashamed of the deed. 7. We pity that man. 8. I am ashamed of my carelessness.[5] 9. He pities them. 10. We ought to learn.[6] 11. I ought to worship God. 12. We ought to reverence (our) parents.

[1] Say, it-pities him of the man. [2] Say, it-irks him of life. [3] Say, it-pities me of this boy. [4] Say, it-will-shame him of the deed. [5] Say, it-shames me of my carelessness. [6] Say, it-behoves us to-learn.

EXERCISE XXVIII.

1. We hate the wicked. 2. The men hate us. 3. Bad men hate me. 4. To remember me.[1] 5. To hate the wicked. 6. (Ye) know my friend. 7. (We) shall know your friends. 8. Fare (ye) well.

[1] See § 98.

EXERCISE XXIX.

1. (We) were walking out-of-doors. 2. (He) has written many letters to-day. 3. A deaf man cannot hear.[1] 4. Let him come hither. 5. The boy runs quickly.[2] 6. Let the boys run quickly. 7. (We) have received many letters

to-day, all carefully written. 8. (We) will go into the city again. 9. Where have they laid him?[3] 10. I shall write a letter to-morrow. 11. The soldier fights bravely. 12. This soldier will fight very bravely. 13. Let the soldier fight bravely. 14. This letter is very badly written.

[1] Cannot, is not able, *non potest.*   [2] Quickly, *celeriter.*   [3] See § 129, *b.*

EXERCISE XXX.

1. The king was walking in the garden. 2. (He) has built a house in the city. 3. The soldiers will walk through the city. 4. Let them come to me. 5. Come (ye) into my garden. 6. The master is loved by (his) pupils. 7. They are praised by these; they are blamed by those. 8. (We) will go into the house of the Lord. 9. Farewell, boys.

I

INDEX TO VOCABULARIES.

LATIN WORDS.

---

mansio, 7
manus, 6
mater, 1
melius, 20
mendax, 1, 2
mendico, 24
mensa, 2
mensis, 9
merces, 21
meus, 5
miles, 2
minister, 24
miser, 3
mitto, 15
moneo, 13
mons, 2
mora, 12
mortalis, 7
mucro, 6
mulier, 2
multus, 2
mundus (clean), 25
mundus (world), 5
murus, 1
mustum, 21
muto, 20

N

Nam, 27
nauta, 9
navigo, 9
nec-nec, 15
negligentia, 27
nemo, 13
neque, 25
nescio, 25
nidus, 12
niger, 2
nihil, 25
noceo, 13
nolo, 25
nomen, 1
non, 12
non solum, 12
noster, 5
nox, 4
nubes, 18
nunc, 16
nunquam, 20
nuptiae, 20

O

Obdormio, 18
occidit sol, 26
occido, 19

occisus, 24
oculus, 2
omnis, 1
oneratus, 25
operarius, 21
optimus, 3
opus, 2
oratio, 20
Oriens, 19
oro, 9
ŏs, 19
ovis, 7

P

Palmes, 8
panis, 6, 12
parens, 6
pars, 4
parvus, 2
pasco, 15
pastor, 1
pater, 1
paucus, 12
pauper, 12
pecco, 10
pax, 8
peccatum, 25
per, 10, 15
pessimus, 3
Pilatus, 16
pisciculus, 12
piscis, 24
placeo, 23
planto, 27
plenus, 21
pono, 25
populus, 3
porta, 6
potens, 1
praeceptor, 10
praemium, 5
praetereo, 25
primus, 6
pro, 11
profundus, 2
prohibeo, 25
propheta, 22
propter, 24
puella, 2
puer, 2
pugno, 9
pulcher, 3
punio, 18
purus, 2

Q

Quaero, 23
que, 25
qui, 12
quia, 10, 20, 23
quidam, 5
quis, 9
quo, 16
quod, 27
quomodo, 29
quoniam, 23
quot, 12

R

Recte, 10
reficio, 25
rego, 15
reperio, 23
resurgo, 16
rex, 2
rosa, 4
rota, 6

S

Sacer, 1
sacerdotium, 26
saepe, 20
sal, 7
salvator, 6
sanctus, 11, 19
sanguis, 6
sapiens, 1
sapientia, 6, 24
scio, 18
scriba, 4
scribo, 15
scriptus, 22
se, 15
secundum, 24
secundus, 9
sed, 9, 16
sed etiam, 12
semper, 9
sentio, 18
sepelio, 18
septem, 4, 12
septimus, 9
servus, 19
si, 20
sicut, 16
signum, 5

silva, 15
similiter, 24
sine, 11, 25
sino, 25
sitio, 18
sol, 6
solvo, 25
somniator, 18
somnus, 7
soror, 15
speratus, 20
spero, 10
spes, 5
spiritus, 4
splendidus, 8
stella, 4
stipendia, 20
stultus, 1, 10
suadeo, 23
sub, 13
super, 10, 24
surdus, 18
surgo, 17, 25
sustollo, 25
suus, 5

T

Taceo, 14
tango, 16
templum, 1
tempus, 2

terra, 6
terreo, 21
testis, 2
timeo, 12
timor, 6
tollo, 25
totus, 5
trado, 17
transeo, 25
tres, 4
tulerunt, 25
turba, 26
turbati sunt, 30
tuus, 5

U

Ubi, 8
unde, 26
unquam, 13, 18
unus, 4
urbs, 5
ut, 11
uterque, 5
utilis, 3
uxor, 27

V

Vado, 15
valde, 29

velut, 12
vendo, 27
venio, 18
venturus, 19
ventus, 9
verbum, 5, 25
veritas, 7
verus, 7
vester, 5
vestio, 23
via, 2
victoria, 20
victus, 22
video, 12
vigesimus, 9
vigilia, 30
vigilo, 11
vinco, 15
vinum, 1
vir, 1
virgo, 9
virtus, 6, 24
vita, 1
vitia, 7
vivens, 26
vivo, 17
vivus, 8
voco, 9
volo (fly), 9
volucris, 12
voluntas, 24
vox, 5
vulpes, 12

JOHN HEYWOOD, Excelsior Printing and Stationery Works, Hulme Hall Road, Manchester.

SCIENCE LECTURES FOR THE PEOPLE.

THIRD AND FOURTH SERIES.

Seventeen Lectures, delivered in Manchester. Crown 8vo, cloth, 2s. 6d. The Third Series may be had in Stiff Paper Cover, price 9d. The Fourth Series may also be had in Stiff Paper Cover, with Portrait of Faraday, price 1s.

Third Series.—One Penny each.

YEAST. By Professor Huxley, LL.D., F.R.S.

COAL COLOURS. By Professor Roscoe, F.R.S.

ON THE ORIGIN OF THE ENGLISH PEOPLE. By Professor Wilkins, M.A.

FOOD FOR PLANTS. By Professor Odling, F.R.S.

THE UNCONSCIOUS ACTION OF THE BRAIN. By Dr. Carpenter, F.R.S.

ON EPIDEMIC DELUSIONS. By Dr. Carpenter, F.R.S.

ON THE PROGRESS OF SANITARY SCIENCE. By Prof. Roscoe, F.R.S.

Fourth Series.—One Penny each.

THE RAINBOW. By Professor Roscoe, F.R.S.

THE ICE AGE IN BRITAIN. By Professor Geikie, F.R.S.

THE SUN AND THE EARTH. By Prof. Balfour Stewart, F.R.S.

ATOMS. By Professor Clifford, M.A., of Cambridge.

FLAME. By Professor Core.

THE LIFE OF FARADAY. By Dr. J. H. Gladstone, F.R.S.

THE STAR DEPTHS. By R. A. Proctor, Esq., F.R.A.S.

KENT CAVERN. By William Pengelly, Esq., F.R.S.

ELECTRICAL DISCOVERIES OF FARADAY. By W. F. Barrett, Esq.

ANCIENT AND MODERN EGYPT; or, THE PYRAMIDS AND THE SUEZ CANAL. By Dr. Carpenter, F.R.S.

SCIENCE LECTURES FOR THE PEOPLE.

Fifth Series.—Eight Lectures delivered in Manchester. Crown 8vo, Stiff Paper Cover, with Portrait of Liebig, 10d.—One Penny each.

POLARISATION OF LIGHT. By William Spottiswoode, Esq., F.R.S.

FERTILISATION OF FLOWERS. By A. W. Bennett, Esq., M.A., B.Sc., F.L.S.

PARASITES. By T. Spencer Cobbold, Esq., M.D., F.R.S.

GUN COTTON. By F. A. Abel, Esq., F.R.S., Royal Arsenal, Woolwich.

ANIMAL MECHANICS. By S. M. Bradley, Esq., F.R.C.S.

THE SENSES. By Professor G. Croom Robertson, M.A.

ON MUSCLE AND NERVE. By Professor Gamgee, M.D., F.R.S.

THE TIME THAT HAS ELAPSED SINCE THE ERA OF THE CAVE MEN OF DEVONSHIRE. By Wm. Pengelly, Esq., F.R.S.

There is no better means of
than the study of **Algebra**;
subjects for which simple arit
ject an interest and importanc
Subject Series of Class Boo
will meet the requirements of
rally in Elementary schools,
Algebraic Test Cards furni
the conduct of various operatio
Elementary School Algebr
   the New Code. Enlarged,
   By HENRY TAYLOR. Sewe
   " A cheap elementary introd
   "This work has been compil
Educational Code. It contains
equations, with full exercises a
master.
   " The Algebra is a sensible lit
Code."—*Papers for the Schoolma*
Algebraic Test Cards, for Sta
   In Three Packets; each co
   Answers on a separate Card
Algebra. One of the "Extra S
   IV., V., and VI., of the
   MAJOR, B.A. In Three Part
   sewed; cloth limp, 8d.
Outlines of Algebra. Witl
   Elementary Schools. By W
   "This is a little twopenny intro
for Elementary Schools where A
ples are easy, and well chosen to
pupil up to the cube root, and int
simple equations."—*School Board*
   "Cheap, well-intentioned, and
   "Is perhaps the cheapest book
can confidently recommend it."—

Politica

Those who take the subject of
New Code, we refer to our work in
adapted to the Three Standards.
Political Economy. One of the "
   for Standards IV., V., and VI. o
   H. MAJOR, B.A. In Three P
   plete, 9d.; cloth limp, 1s.
   "We have much pleasure in re
books."—*Victoria Magazine,* August,
   " We are astonished to see how ski
important branch of study have be
and yet leaves room here and there f
the reader, and enable him to grasp t
Board Chronicle, July 13, 1872.
   "Mr. Sn ith's definitions and expla

Algebra.

There is no better means of strengthening a pupil's grasp of Arithmetic than the study of **Algebra**; but the facilities it affords for dealing with subjects for which simple arithmetic is wholly inadequate, give the subject an interest and importance of its own. The **Algebra** in the **Extra Subject Series of Class Books**, or the **Elementary School Algebra**, will meet the requirements of the several Standards, and of pupils generally in Elementary schools, while the **Outlines of Algebra** and the **Algebraic Test Cards** furnish exercises by which the pupil's skill in the conduct of various operations may be readily tested.

Elementary School Algebra (The), for Standards IV., V., and VI. of the New Code. Enlarged, revised, and corrected. (Second Edition.) By HENRY TAYLOR. Sewed, 6d.; cloth limp, 8d.
" A cheap elementary introduction."—*Athenæum.*
"This work has been compiled to meet the requirements of the New Educational Code. It contains the elements of Algebra as far as simple equations, with full exercises and clear explanations."—*National Schoolmaster.*
" The Algebra is a sensible little book, and well suited to meet the New Code."—*Papers for the Schoolmaster.*

Algebraic Test Cards, for Standards IV., V., and VI. of the New Code. In Three Packets; each containing 80 Exercises on 20 Cards, with Answers on a separate Card. By HENRY TAYLOR. 6d. per packet.

Algebra. One of the "Extra Subject" Series of Class Books for Standards IV., V., and VI., of the New Code By DR. SNAITH and H. MAJOR, B.A. In Three Parts. F'cap 8vo, 2d. each. Complete, 6d.; sewed; cloth limp, 8d.

Outlines of Algebra. With Examples and Exercises for use in Elementary Schools. By W. CHITTY. Sewed, 2d.
"This is a little twopenny introduction to Algebra, intended principally for Elementary Schools where Algebra is an 'extra' subject. The examples are easy, and well chosen to illustrate the rules. The book takes the pupil up to the cube root, and introduces him to the manipulation of very simple equations."—*School Board Chronicle*, July 6, 1872.
"Cheap, well-intentioned, and useful."—*Ed. Reporter*, July, 1872.
"Is perhaps the cheapest book on Algebra published. * * * * We can confidently recommend it."—*National Schoolmaster*, July, 1872.

Political Economy.

Those who take the subject of **Political Economy**, as given in the New Code, we refer to our work in the "Extra Subject" Series, which is adapted to the Three Standards.

Political Economy. One of the "Extra Subject" Series of Class Books for Standards IV., V., and VI. of the New Code. By Dr. SNAITH and H. MAJOR, B.A. In Three Parts. F'cap 8vo, 3d. each. Complete, 9d.; cloth limp, 1s.
"We have much pleasure in recommending these excellent class books."—*Victoria Magazine*, August, 1872.
" We are astonished to see how skilfully the salient points of this most important branch of study have been compressed into so small a space, and yet leaves room here and there for illustration which will interest the reader, and enable him to grasp the principles more firmly."—*School Board Chronicle*, July 13, 1872.
"Mr. Snaith's definitions and explanations are good."—*Athenæum.*

www.ingramcontent.com/pod-product-compliance
Ingram Content Group UK Ltd.
Pitfield, Milton Keynes, MK11 3LW, UK
UKHW020748300125
454332UK00008B/303